Between You and Me

NINTH

H. M. QUEEN ELIZABETH THE QUEEN MOTHER FELLOWSHIP

Between You and Me

Closing the gap between people and health care

JESSICA CORNER

The Nuffield Trust

FOR RESEARCH AND POLICY
STUDIES IN HEALTH SERVICES

London: The Stationery Office

The Nuffield Trust

The Nuffield Trust for research and policy studies in health services was established by Viscount Nuffield in 1940. Today the Trust acts as an independent commentator on the UK health scene and the National Health Service. It has set out to illuminate current issues through informed debate, meetings and publications; and has also commissioned research and policy studies aimed at the development of policy and improvement of health services.

Address;
59 New Cavendish Street,
London
W1M 7RD, UK

Tel: 020 7631 8450
Fax: 020 7631 8451

Email: mail@nuffieldtrust.org.uk
Internet: http://www.nuffieldtrust.org.uk

HER MAJESTY QUEEN ELIZABETH THE QUEEN MOTHER FELLOWSHIP

Her Majesty Queen Elizabeth the Queen Mother, who is the Patron of the Trust and has always shown a keen interest in its work, approved the founding of the Fellowship by the Trust to commemorate her 80th birthday.

The Trustees of The Nuffield Trust will select a Fellow who will be invited to undertake a review in a monograph of a subject within the sphere of the Trust which is believed to be of particular interest to Her Majesty. The monograph will be launched by a lecture.

ABOUT THE AUTHOR

Professor Jessica Corner was born in Alderbury, near Salisbury, Wiltshire in 1961, and grew up on a farm near Stonehenge. She studied for a degree in Nursing at Chelsea College, London University. After working as a staff nurse in Cardiothoracic care at St George's Hospital, Tooting, she trained as a Cancer nurse at the Royal Marsden Hospital. Following a short spell working as a research assistant in the Nursing Education Research Unit at King's College, she commenced her doctoral research there into the attitudes and experiences of newly qualified nurses in caring for people with cancer. She was appointed Macmillan lecturer in cancer and palliative care at King's College in 1988. In 1990, having completed her doctorate, she moved to the Institute of Cancer Research and Royal Marsden Hospital to establish an Academic Nursing Unit. She was appointed Director of the Centre for Cancer and Palliative Care Studies at the Institute in 1994, and Professor of Cancer Nursing in 1996 at the age of 35. Her outside interests are, her two daughters born 12 years apart, escaping London to the Lake District and Dorset, and her flute.

ACKNOWLEGEMENTS

My sincere thanks to Sir Kenneth Stowe for his friendship, wise counsel and help in preparing the monograph; to Charlie Westbury for our lunches at Tui's, his encouragement over the years and for finding some of the material for the monograph; to Anne Marie Rafferty, Sally Redfern and David Clark for their helpful comments on my early drafts; to Fotini Ash for her practical help and support in researching the monograph and in its production; finally, to John Wyn Owen and the Nuffield Trust for inviting me to undertake the Fellowship and involving me in the Trust's many activities while gathering my thoughts, it has been inspiring, and an education.

For Chris, Millie and Edie,

and

Bunny and Judy.

Contents

Foreword   xiii

1. Introduction   1

2. Between You and Me   4

3. Medicalised Lives?   14

4. The Professions   25

5. Architectures of Treatment   36

6. 'Me'   46

7. Conclusions   61

References   63

Foreword

The Queen Mother Fellowship is both an immense honour and a challenge (a challenge for which I feel almost entirely lacking in qualification). Although I strive to be never far away from the immediacy of people in need of care and continue to participate in caring, I have not spent years at the coal-face, beside the bed or in the clinic, demonstrating my qualification through the straightforward act of 'doing' health care. I am both an insider and an outsider of health care, deeply committed and at the same time deeply troubled by what I see and experience; choosing to place myself and my work not quite on the outside and not quite on the inside. I am also a nurse, and as such I am exempt from high office and the demands of producing a major scientific breakthrough in curing disease.

The status of 'exempt' from high influence, has certain advantages; in particular being free to tackle the seemingly obscure, less grand in scale, matters of health care. My interest here, therefore, is to explore in some detail a small, even mundane, aspect of care and treatment; that is the central relationship between health care as it is practised and the people who have need of it. My argument will be, that where we erode or undermine this relationship, and health care seems to be singularly destined to do so, all the ambitions, good intentions, humanity, values, indeed even the ability to achieve the very goals of health care, also fail. As I will argue, if inherent failure in this relationship is somehow enshrined in health care, then we must examine why this is so? And, how this came to be?

The invitation to speak and write coming at the beginning of the new millennium demands some millennial thoughts on health care. However, in keeping with those authors most influential to me, my thoughts do not immediately turn to the future, to a new utopia where all that is wrong currently may be made right as we discover the means to overcome the problems I might identify. Rather, it is a moment in which to pause, and reflect, reflect on the great twentieth century project of the Western world, health and freedom from disease for all, provided by the great advances of scientific and medical discovery. I am rather taken by Frederic Jameson's term 'inverted millenarianism', brought to my attention by Neil Leach's 'Rethinking Architecture', a theme I shall pursue later in relation to health care, whereby a new realism about such grand projects as the crude and simplistic notion that scientific progress can overcome all that may threaten global health, is adopted. Inversion suggests a more reflective stance. Instead of predicting the future, more is to be learnt from reflecting backwards, since through this one may understand what is required in order to effect change (Leach 1997).

I have chosen a series of themes in which I explore how the relationship between health care and those in need of it operates and is experienced; also how and why in many instances health care erodes or undermines this relationship. These themes are selective rather than all encompassing; they illustrate the fact that there is no simple solution to the problems I highlight. The knowledge system, the people who provide care and treat disease, and the environment of health care, all contribute to its experience. My writing here is a collection of related essays that explore these themes, rather than a single unified text. I must, therefore, apologise for asking readers to make some of the connections for themselves.

At times I may take what will seem a polemical stance. I do so in order to make clear to the reader the problems I highlight and to maintain my argument. I have drawn on material from a wide range of sources, these act as narratives of the experience of health care and thereby illuminate or offer a form of evidence for my argument. I have not explicitly directed my writing at health policy or attempted to underpin statements with detailed evidence, although this certainly exists. I have chosen to take a different tack, to focus on getting the questions that need to be raised right, and not to find the answers. Finally, I make a tentative recommendation for a more concerted effort to be made to incorporate 'self' and care of people's 'selves' into health care.

1. Introduction

There are many challenges in providing 21st century health care. Disease still rages; poverty and inequity still represent the greatest threats to global health; and paradoxically science and its industries are responsible for the most significant man-made causes of disease and the promise of eventual elimination of much of what we now understand as disease. Setting aside these grand themes, the problem I wish to explore is the experience of health care, which all too frequently is deeply unsatisfactory and yet has received little attention in attempts to reform health care.

Although there is a laudable drive to re-organise health care delivery and make patients' concerns central to this (DOH 2000) the current themes in the debate about mechanisms for enhancing health care, such as health service funding, evidence-based health care, or governance do not address the experience of health care directly, nor will for example the recent injection of significant funding increases into health care necessarily address it. The problem is more fundamental. Despite high profile cases of medical negligence, treatment by and large is given where required, the public's health, although it could be much improved, is largely adequate, and certainly much better than a century ago. What lies at the heart of the unsatisfactory aspects of health care is something different. It is much more personal.

Our encounters with health care as 'patients', or perhaps as the relative or friend of someone receiving treatment or care, seem to be coloured by a feeling that we as people don't matter. We become objects to be processed, our health problems dealt with, eventually, but adopted by the health care system as entities separate from ourselves. Once the health problem is processed, we find ourselves ejected back to our normal lives. Little or no connection exists between the acts of health care and what is normal or what matters to us.

A gap exists between health care and ourselves, a gap designed to be occupied by things, not designed to be about me the person who is ill or in need of care, but about health care and health care functions. The 'system', the processes and procedures that seem to dominate, the physical structures of health care – buildings, machines, equipment, the people engaged in administering the system, the way matters relating to health care are communicated - are all about 'you' – the person in charge of my care or treatment, or about the administration of a vast bureaucracy. They are not about 'me' – the person for whom the processes and procedures are designed. Nowhere does there appear to be effort directed at examining and enhancing the experience of health care by those who receive it.

My purpose here is to explore (by posing and attempting to answer a series of questions) the experience of health care, then to examine some key themes in relation to why health care enshrines practices that exclude the sense of being cared for as a person. This exclusion has arisen because the knowledge base used in treating disease is derived from a tradition that treats personal experience as unnecessary and is therefore not taken into account in encounters with patients. The health professions have marked out profession specific territories such that personal care has been relegated to the status of low level and unimportant work. The physical environment of health care, the buildings and interior design, reinforce the disciplinary authority of health professionals and exclude self-action by people in relation to their health. Alone, each of these influences might be relatively unimportant, together, they create a vast immovable system, dominated by lack of attention to personalising care, a system that resists reform and obscures insight into aspects of health care that require fundamental overhaul. Becoming conscious of the building blocks of impersonal care and the origins of these is the first step in orchestrating change.

Health care is not a static entity. It constantly evolves and changes; so too does the relationship between the system and the people within it. Recently attempts have been made to give people (or rather patients) greater involvement in determining health care. One aspect of emergent change within health care is a progressive recognition of the need to attend to 'the patient's' concerns. Variously, models such as quality assurance, which, among other activities, takes service users' views into account and catalogues and attends to complaints, have been adopted. Other attempts have been made to recreate, within new models of service organisation, the patient a passive figure, into a 'consumer' or 'user', an individual who makes choices and expresses dissatisfaction. In the most recent and perhaps ultimate reform the patient as service 'user' is recast as an insider and engaged in the processes of making decisions about the shape of services. Others have addressed more directly personal relationships, and have recognised the need to train doctors and other health professionals in the skills of communicating with patients. These laudable projects are, over time, having an important effect and will allow us to realise a very different system and experience of care. Although, media reporting of many incidents where the recipients of care have been grossly neglected suggests that attempts at change have, thus far, at best only been partially effective.

High profile cases where hospitals and professionals have been criticised for neglecting aspects of personal care and the fact that greater attention is being given to individuals who express their feelings about their treatment, means that health care is under pressure to change. Understanding that evolution is happening and that this might be harnessed and promoted rather than resisted, might in time allow the creation of a health care system that is more responsive and personal in its attentions to those in need of it. The change that is needed is not necessarily structural. In the past too often health service reorganisations have occurred through adopting a 'grand design' approach. Change is imposed using a new ogranisational structure, usually determined centrally and applied throughout the health service, implying new roles, responsibilities and management hierarchies. Promoting and shaping health care for the future could instead be through mechanisms that address fundamental values or issues, and these may be much more successful than the 'grand design' approach so familiar in National Health Service reform.

In examining the reasons why health care is experienced as impersonal I will explore a unifying idea, a value, which might direct change and help assist a more attentive and inclusive health care system to be devised. A system that acknowledges personal experiences in health care and also actively harnesses these so that people are enabled to maintain greater control over their health and over illness. I want to suggest care of the 'self' as this value, and to argue that this should be adopted as a central tenet of health care. Also, how the structures of health care might be refashioned in order to make care of people's 'selves' a practical reality.

2. Between You and Me

Why is the space between you, the health carer or health care system, and me the person in need of treatment or care so great and occupied by things that are designed to be for your benefit, and not mine?

I have for the purposes of illustration three stories, two from real life and one fictional and humorous.

Sarah Cutler(1996) in *A Survivor's Tale* tells of the experience of her partner's care in a North American state-of-the-art teaching hospital. This account suggests that while there may be particular problems with our UK system these may pervade health care more generally. Sarah's partner Mike was admitted after developing weakness in his arms and legs and was found to have an inoperable brain tumour. The story spans several months and begins after Mike is admitted via the emergency department. The account details how they wait several days for the biopsy to be reported:

'Shocked and terrified, we wait, the hours crawl. From time to time a nurse checks Mike's blood pressure. With a flash of gallows humour, he jokes that the concern for his blood pressure is misplaced since he knows what he is dying of! Our nerves are jangled by the incessant clamour of a call bell located just outside our door. At wits' end and with an edge in my voice, I ask a man at the nursing station about the disturbance. "Nothing you need worry about," he snarls. His reply is intended to set my boundaries. It sets a tone. We resume our dreary vigil. …Sunday evening a nurse reveals again the biopsy might be postponed; in the meantime , a doctor has suggested that the mass might be an infection rather than a tumour. Only a biopsy will tell. Teased by hope and starved of information, we have by Sunday night endured a lifetime of suspense.

…Monday morning the nursing supervisor returns after a four-day absence to reports of my distress. She asks to speak to me. "Sally" she begins, " I want you to know that I too, have grown children." Momentarily unbalanced, I quickly realise she thinks I am Mike's mother! I laugh.

Later on, the radiation oncologist, for reasons unclear to me remarks "At least we know Mike has some sort of family out there".

"How's the girl friend today?" asks a primary nurse. Our unconventional relationship seems to excite speculation and gratuitous comment laced with disapproval. I feel slightly defensive for the first time in our years together.

To nearly everyone we are "Mike" and "Sally". Despite his doctorate in physics and a long resumé of professional achievements, Mike is degraded and infantilised. Only once does a physician invite the use of her familiar name. While doctors younger than my children stand over his helpless body, Mike stoically endures their mock-cheerful greetings.

Two or three days after the biopsy confirms our darkest fears, Mike begins twice daily radiotherapy: this means travelling by wheelchair, later by trolley, down several floors to the basement of another building. There he will wait his turn among other miserable human beings in various stages of debilitation. Some speak in hushed tones with relatives whose faces are creased with worry. Others, more dead than alive, lie mute and hollow-eyed on trolleys.

…to arrive at this scene of desolation we rely on the round-trip services of porters. Since demand exceeds supply, patients ready to return to their rooms sometimes sit or lie wretchedly for as long as an hour before they are rescued. As Mike's condition swiftly deteriorates these delays cost him nearly unbearable physical and emotional torment.

On Mike's last day of radiation, I wait in vain for a wheelchair. Finally I ask the man at the desk to find one for us. Twenty minutes pass and no wheelchair appears. I return to him to suggest that he telephone the radiotherapy department to explain our delay. "By the way" I say "is the wheelchair on the way?" The man who had told me to mind my own business the first time we met fires back "I've ordered the wheelchair and it will be here when it gets here!"

Early one morning I find Mike's door closed. The nurse in the hall asks me to wait outside while Mike uses the commode. Moments later she peers through the window and exclaims with evident dismay. "Oh my goodness he's fallen on the floor" …the profound humiliation Mike must have felt at finding himself naked on the floor and powerless to recover. We have reached a very low point. Afterwards the nurse says, "Well now we know he can't be left unattended."

...It is mid-November. I request a private meeting with Mike's physician to question whether the radiation treatments, which are clearly compounding Mike's distress, should continue. He persuades me to proceed.

In retrospect, I rue that decision. Knowing what I now know, I believe the outlook was hopeless from the beginning.... But our need for truth competes with the physician's need to battle the cancer, however hopeless the odds and at whatever the costs – physical, emotional, and financial- to the patient. He woos me with graphs and hypotheses, I allow myself to be seduced.

Our ability for our physician to accept defeat gracefully is dramatised in our last meeting, which has all the marks of a hit–and-run accident. Shortly before noon on a day in December he comes into Mike's room to speak with me. Leading me to the elevator area where there is no place to sit, he delivers his message. "We're stopping radiation. It's not doing any good. I have a meeting to go to." Without another word he vanishes into a waiting elevator. We will never see or hear from him again.

We pack up and come home. We have seen the last of hospitals. (Cutler S 1997 p 37-40)

An everyday tale of health care, replicated daily in our own health service. Inhumanity is enshrined in the hospital system; it is reflected in the myriad incidents of carelessness and seemingly trivial aspects of care that are neglected. Mike is progressively reduced from the status of renowned and effective scientist, to that of an infant. While his illness will reduce him functionally in this way, the health care system and all who work in it, from ward clerical assistant to consultant oncologist, will add materially to his loss of dignity and physical and mental competence.

Encounters with health care, brief or long, are characterised by an unfolding relationship between the health care system and the person who needs it. Most often and most importantly encounters revolve around interactions with personnel, for example: a telephone call to a general practitioner's receptionist; a consultation with a doctor over troubling symptoms; a series of tests or investigations; having to relinquish one's bodily functions to nurses because of serious illness or following an operation; decisions communicated by a medical specialist about how a serious illness is to be managed. Encounters also take place within a physical environment: the hospital outpatient department or ward, the general practitioner's surgery, the accident and emergency department. Although many of the examples I use are from hospital environments, the problems are not confined to these. They are pervasive throughout and are also found in encounters with health care within community settings. Together, the relationships with those delivering health care and the environment where treatment and care take place create our experiences of it. These experiences punctuate our lives, from the mundane to the monumental moments of life: birth, illness and death, as in *A Survivor's Tale*. Too often, encounters with health care are deeply impersonal and unsatisfactory, and one is left with the impression that there has been a distinct lack of personal care. Yet health policy and the many reorganisations of our UK health service have in general not been directed towards these experiences of health care.

Despite massive investment by successive governments, our health care system has a utilitarian and impersonal feel about it. After more than a decade of promoting consumerism, the real needs of people, the sense of 'me' being cared for, still seems absent. The Ombudsman's reports are testimony to this; an analysis of themes from these reports yields important insights into what goes wrong. Complaints to the Ombudsman are frequently not about failure to give adequate treatment, although this is of course important, and the subject of much current interest given recent high profile legal actions. They reveal instead a litany of:

- delays in treatment;

- important decisions and care left to junior members of staff inadequately trained or competent to deal with the situation;

- a lack of attention to detail in ensuring that service is maintained continuously;

- there is insensitivity and thoughtlessness in relation to people;

- a tendency for staff to retreat into bureaucratic structures rather than being thoughtful over what is needed;

- a defensive closed shop posture by senior managers;

- barriers imposed by the rigidly hierarchical structure of the NHS;

- delays and avoidance in the handling of complaints (HMSO 1998).

Patient satisfaction surveys in contrast reveal high rates of satisfaction, but do they do more than reveal what low expectations of health care the public has?

My second story is an excerpt from a personal view written for the British Medical Journal by Clare Hamon, called *Witnessing poor care either brutalises you or outrages you*. She writes:

'During the Christmas period of 1997, Simon, the husband of a good friend of mine, died in hospital, 12 days after his admission and nine days after major surgery. During his hospital stay two other patients died in his bay of the ward. One was in the bed next to Simon. In the few hours before his death he was incontinent of faeces six times. The man found this distressing and repeatedly apologised. Although a nurse cleaned him up each time, his body was left on the ward for two hours after his death, during which time Simon was aware of the strong smell of his faeces. It would have been preferable for this man to have died in a single cubicle, but none was available. Witnessing his distress and loss of dignity must have been terrible and worrying for the other inpatients.

The body of the other man was left on the ward for an hour and a half after his death. When his wife came in, no nurse was around, and she threw her arms around Simon for comfort, an experience for which he was unfit, physically and emotionally.

A man with Alzheimer's disease was in a bed opposite Simon. He kept pulling out his catheter and he had blood all over his pyjamas. When my friend told a nurse about this, her reply indicated that it was expected that the other patients would look after him. He was very disturbed that night. Simon and another patient resorted to sleeping in the day room. Another patient was so upset by the man with Alzheimer's that he discharged himself and drove home, 250 miles away, just 24 hours after his operation.'

(Hamon C 1998, p1463)

Simon and his fellow roommates are characterised by their lack of ability to act on behalf of themselves, not simply because they are very sick, and in fact dying, but because for some reason they feel unable to make simple requests that might enhance their well-being. Like Goffman's (1968) inmates of the total institution, resistance is not possible and not attempted. While their bodies are declining, they themselves have undergone a more profound 'mortification', that of the loss of their sense of self through the degradation imposed by the kind of experiences the account implies. One man escapes like a prisoner 'on the run'.

Many of the reasons why health care has developed in this way are historical. Biomedicine as a dominant determinant of how health care is constructed, has been highly influential in the organisation and work of the health service. Remnants of nineteenth century poor laws remain in the health service culture. The national health service as a publicly funded service institutionalised a particular kind of contract between the doctor or health professional and the person in need of care; social control rather than a customer/service relationship dominates. Health professionals have been socialised into roles that value adherence to a system rationed by time as well as by money over the needs of the individual. Professional roles in health care have been determined along rigidly gendered lines, now out of step with wider social changes. Hospital architecture and institutional structures also reflect this historical legacy. These problems are not simply about how a single professional group, such as doctors, organises the way it works. They are inherent. They suffuse throughout.

Hospitals and health care processes are dominated by procedures encased in a vast inflexible bureaucratic structure. Information, thought to be liberating in our electronic age, is rigidly controlled and largely withheld from people within the system, and yet at the same time, outside the formal system health knowledge is a burgeoning industry of health related products and lifestyle advice. Care and treatment processes are organised for the convenience of institutions and doctors, rather than for ease of use or access. People become infants in the system, and care is characterised by mistakes, delays and inefficiency. Worst of all there is an apparent inability of staff to 'see' what distresses.

My final story was told by Frank Muir, as part of his *A Kentish Lad* memoirs for BBC Radio 4. In order to fully appreciate the joke one has to picture Frank Muir and his inimitable delivery:

'A man needed lower (shall we say) abdominal surgery. He had an insurance plan, so went privately for his operation. When he got to University Hospital private patient room, he did what the notice told him to…Took off all his clothes, lay on a hard trolley thing and covered his lower half with a towel.

After waiting about an hour there was a knock at the door

"come in" he said.

A nurse came in and said "I shall prepare you for your operation now".

She went over to the sink, picked up a razor and said I shall have to shave you for your operation…she whisked off the towel…then proceeded to shave him…relevantly…. Then she picked up a bottle of surgical spirit, and proceeded to daub him with this on his freshly, scraped, raw, shaven skin.

Afterwards she told him to get up, and while he stood there she slipped him into a green back to front surgical gown.

Then she said "before I walk you round to theatre for your operation, is there anything you wish to ask me?"

… "Yes" he said … "Why did you knock?"

The common courtesy of knocking before entering someone's private-room amongst all the other assaults on personal dignity and privacy seems so misplaced as to be comical.

You will notice that the stories I have selected do not feature a single professional group, or setting of care, or condition. Nothing and no one escapes responsibility for the failure within health care to attend to a sense of 'me'. It is the easiest of dimensions of care and treatment to be neglected, under pressure it is the first to be abandoned, and it is the first to be felt as poor care.

It is the dynamics between the collective of health care 'you', and the person who needs care 'me', which require reform. Health care needs refocusing, to direct greater attention toward 'me' and my concerns. This implies a refocusing of health policy away from conventional organisational and structural issues towards a closer attention to the relationship between health carers and health care as a collective endeavour, with individuals and their particular needs.

This may seem an overwhelmingly negative view of contemporary health care; much has changed and is changing for the better. Many of the recent policy reforms have sought to resolve problems, for example a new agenda for quality has been set (DOH 1998) as well as a re-invigorated obligation to address patients' concerns and involve patients as 'users' of health care in many areas of decision-making and planning (DOH 2000). These are important and will influence the delivery of care. However, policy in future needs to directly address ways of refocusing health care on:

- the way it might be tailored to how individuals want it;

- how to make accessing health care services less disruptive to normal life;

- how the distress and difficulty of ill health might be acknowledged directly by those involved in providing health care.

This is the beginning of a new era, not simply defined through the artificiality of date and time, but because we are at a moment in history when all is change; social structures, relationships, institutions and even whole societies are altering as never before. The patient of 20 years ago no doubt had fewer expectations of personalised treatment than today; more passive and more likely to accept any advice or recommendation made by a doctor or nurse without question. In 20 years from now users of health services will be very different from today; able to access a variety of forms of health care information and provision through the internet and other media. They will be better informed, more selective in what they will choose to access from formal health care, and much more likely to question medical authority (Dargie 1999). The imperative to consider mechanisms for change therefore is not simply a matter of addressing a system that is currently inadequate. Failure to act may have grave consequences. An additional pressure will arise with the 1998 Human Rights Act since there is an obligation to accommodate new rights. It is for these very reasons that it is timely to consider the possibility of refocusing health care both to preserve the values of personal care for people within a vast and pressured system, but also to overhaul and overthrow, where necessary, the inadequacies of the present.

'This is not to engage in some game of 'deconstruction', nor to delegitimate that which we take to be pure by revealing its ' impure' origins. Rather, in revealing the complex contingencies that have made up the territory we inhabit and the horizons of our experience, in showing that things could have been different, such analyses encourage us to weigh up the costs as well as the benefits of the present we inhabit. They thus allow us to dream of a time in which our times could be different again'. Nikolas Rose (1994, p71).

3. Medicalised Lives?

Why has biomedicine become invested with so much power over people who are ill and why are more equal relationships with doctors and other health professionals so difficult to achieve?

In the stories I have used in the preceding pages I have been careful to underplay the role of doctors in the problems I outline. Not because I think that doctors do not play a significant part in attending to the sense of 'me' in health care (in fact they have a pivotal role) but because the current debate about medical dominance and power restricts debate to problems associated with a single professional group. Real as these problems are, my argument is with health care as a whole: the procedures and processes in the system, the institutions, the practices, the people. These collectively can be represented by the term 'biomedicine' or for that matter health care. There is, however, an extensive and well rehearsed critique of medicine and medical power and its influences on society as a whole. Many of these arguments could also be read as a critique of biomedicine and health care (see for example Lupton 1994).

Zola (1972,1973), among many others, has been critical of the dominance of medicine in society to the extent that society itself, and therefore our lives, have become medicalised. Medicine has become a major instrument of social control.

According to Zola there is almost no area of life not now seen as a proper object of medicine, especially since the adoption of a multi-causal model of disease. Legislation that restricts the use of surgical procedures and the prescribing of drugs to medical practitioners means that as the effectiveness of these increases and list of interventions and therapeutic agents expands, so too the jurisdiction of medicine expands. The extent of this is such that anything that can be described as an illness will immediately become the object of medical intervention and control: criminality, pregnancy and sexual activity have all come under the extending domain of medicine. For Zola one consequence of this is that disorder is omnipresent, and as the management of such disorder resides with a single group (doctors), then this group is in a position to (and is obliged to) exercise great control and influence over what we should, and should not do. The goal is to prevent or deal with illness and thus enable us to stay healthy. The influence of doctors has largely, until recently, remained unquestioned and unproblematised since medical orderliness or 'health' has become a 'paramount value' in society.

Ivan Illich (1976) suggests that such medicalization of our lives undermines the capacity of people to take care of themselves. Medicine has become a commodity and its availability increases demand for it, which in no direct way relates to need for health care. The result is that where previously individuals might have had resources to cope with illness themselves, this capacity has increasingly been replaced by medically led disease 'management'. Women's health and psychiatric illness have been identified as subject to redefinition and control following medical encroachment on territory previously managed respectively by lay or penal systems. This spread in the power and influence of medicine bears no direct relationship to its success in treating disease and has occurred despite the problems of treatment related side- effects.

Along with technological advances in the management of disease has come an institutionalisation of the socially controlling role of medicine. The process of medicalization and its effects can be seen at a clinical level in the way medical conditions that in a previous era may have been seen as natural problems, have been appropriated by medicine. In society, individuals, families and communities have become deprived of the conditions that provided the capacity for control of their own health and environment: control now rests outside of themselves. Culturally, medicalization 'saps' the ability of people to sustain themselves through the suffering their lives may bring, such as pain, impairment, decline and death.

A more direct effect of medicalization is upon the nature of the relationship between individuals who are sick and encounters with doctors. The rise of the importance of medicine also gives doctors power and status in their role in treating the sick. People who are sick are required to subject themselves to the investigations and ministrations of the medical system in order to get well; in turn they rely on medical care to relieve their suffering since society no longer possesses self-agency in this domain. Within the medical encounter an unequal relationship exists: the doctor is powerful and the person who becomes the patient submits to the doctor's observations and recommendations about treatment. The unequal nature of this relationship has led some people to conclude that too much power is invested in medical authority.

However, to see the problems of medicalization as simply a situation whereby too much power has become invested in medicine and doctors, does not address the central question here, except to acknowledge imbalance in the relationship between doctor and patient, and the enormous influence medicine has on our lives. In order to examine the relationship between biomedicine and the impersonal nature of health care it is necessary to take a step back and continue to use writings from social history, sociology and medical anthropology. These disciplines have thrown open health care for critical examination. Yet much of this work remains at the margins, used only in the study of health care and its practices by academics. These disciplines are of fundamental importance to both the understanding of the problems I raise and to their resolution or reform.

The writing of Michel Foucault, a social scientist and historian of ideas, is arguably central to the developing critique of health care, in particular in the insights he offers into how a study of the past can also be a study of the present (Foucault's *Genealogy*), because the past is ever visible in current health care practices: *'It is a method that has an explicit theoretical and political goal: to disrupt the taken-for- grantedness of the present and show how things could be different' (Bunton and Peterson 1997 p3-4).* This is the task I also set myself here.

Foucault's writing spans a wide range of subjects, and while he focused his attention on a single model of health care in Paris, his writing has wide relevance and can be taken into other settings. Foucault's contribution lies in his refusal to accept history, and the development of reason attributed to the Enlightenment, as necessarily positive, or possible to trace as an incrementally developing series of ideas, events and influences. Indeed Foucault's work suggests that the effect of developments in knowledge and reason was to legitimise power rather than challenge it, and such power became located and maintained in institutions:

'schools, prisons, reformatories, psychiatric facilities, which, though often promoted in the name of 'improvement', in reality consolidated administrative authority,

bureaucratic regulation and […] social control' (Jones and Porter, 1994, *p2*). Accordingly Foucault's work and the many scholars who take forward these perspectives, enable us to see developments in science, medicine and health care not as 'advances' or 'breakthroughs', but as temporary expressions of knowledge or power that have repercussions today (Jones and Porter 1994).

Foucault traces the evolution of medicine (and health care) as we know it today, revealing moments, or movements that have transformed how health care is practised in certain critical ways. The effects of such transformations, which most importantly occurred in changes in medicine between the eighteenth and nineteenth centuries, can be traced as important, defining features of our health care system, some of which are crucial in understanding its deficiencies, as well as its enormous potency. In *Discipline and Punish*, Foucault (1975) explains, using Bentham's name for the design for the new model Victorian reformed prison, 'the panopticon', how this most visible structure, whereby all prisoners could be watched from a single central surveillance point within the prison, became dominant within institutions. This was combined with a system of control and punishment that while less physically brutal than earlier regimes in prisons, was no less complete in its demand for submission to authority.

Foucault argues that panoptic or disciplinary power became integral to other institutional systems such as hospitals and asylums. Even today hospitals are designed to maximise the ability to observe the well-being of patients, for example from the 'nurses' station', and the experience of being a patient remains one whereby one is expected to conform to a regime that is based on the relinquishment of control over oneself (exemplified in the stories presented earlier). While at one level the 'panopticon' is an architectural device designed to optimise a building for its intended purpose it serves as a metaphor: 'panopticism' has become suffused through systems of work in institutions and more particularly in health care, as not a physical structure, but as 'surveillance'. The controlling, watching, total presence of medicine, whilst an avowedly benevolent presence, has become permanent and defining of much of health care (Armstrong 1994, 1995). The panoptic architecture and the disciplinary power so clearly mapped out in Foucault's analysis resonates with the images presented in my three stories.

In Foucault's *Madness and Civilisation* (1989) the development of madness as a medical matter is traced from the pre-modern management of insanity to disciplinary power exerted within asylums. Contrary to the view of psychiatry, Foucault's perspective is that this is simply a move from one form of disciplinary power to another. He points out that it is only relatively recently, at the beginning of the nineteenth century, that madness was subsumed under medical authority. Foucault questions the traditionally held view that the moment when this development occurred can be unquestionably described as 'progress'. After the Middle Ages, when leprosy disappeared in Europe, the insane took the part played by lepers and were segregated, and excluded, and banished from cities. In the classical period banishment was replaced by confinement and restraint, as madness became 'unreason', and the paradoxical manifestation of 'non-being'. The insane were chained and confined with criminals, and later in institutions set aside from society so that the danger of contamination could be minimised. Confinement was not used to suppress madness but to eliminate it from the social order, the goal being correction or death.

The mythical stories of the physicians Tuke in York and Pinel in Paris at the beginning of the nineteenth century who ostensibly 'liberated' the insane from their chains and replaced these with a liberal and philanthropic system of medical care in asylums, are questioned. Foucault argues that confinement was replaced by an equally severe regime. In Pinel's case this was a regime of silence, the absence of language, the abasement and confrontation of madness, and a system of perpetual judgement. Madness was punished in the asylum, and the doctor was for the first time the central figure of authority: not because of his medical knowledge but because he exerted control:

'It is thought that Tuke and Pinel opened the asylum to medical knowledge. They did not introduce science, but a personality, whose powers borrowed from science only their disguise, or at most their justification. These powers, by their nature were of a moral and social order; they took root in the madman's minority status, in the insanity of his person, not of his mind. If the medical personage could isolate madness it was not because he knew it, but because he mastered it; and what for positivism would be an image of objectivity was only the other side of this domination.' (Foucault 1989 p271-2)

Foucault also provides an important analysis of medical practice and the means by which medical knowledge is gained and utilised. In *The Birth of the Clinic* (Foucault 1973) the end of the eighteenth century is identified as a critical time in the development of medicine. It is from this point that the modern notion of 'the clinic' originates. The 'clinic' referred to here does not only relate to the physical space in which medical encounters occur (e.g. the hospital), but also the non-physical space in which medical understanding of the person's illness was investigated, elucidated and defined, so that it could be treated. As developments in science and medicine meant that the body was becoming visible internally, a parallel transformation took place in the way that the body was organised in medical thinking. Before this time medicine had worked within a classificatory system. Illnesses were understood in terms of their effects, not as malfunctioning body systems or parts that gave rise to symptoms, and these were also bound up with and inseperable from the person who was sick. Medical treatment was based on developing a picture of these effects in discussion with the sick person, who remained in charge of his or her ailment. The new medicine operated very differently, as disease became understood as originating in mechanisms operating deep inside the body, and as manifesting itself as symptoms. The doctor's role became that of inquisitor, searching out constellations of symptoms and effects, the signs of disease. Thus the person who was ill became the patient, an object of medical study, and the body as medical object became an entity separate from the body as person. Foucault called this phenomenon medical or clinical 'gaze':

'This new structure is indicated by the minute but decisive change, whereby the question 'what is the matter with you?', which the eighteenth-century dialogue between doctor and patients begun…, was replaced by that other question: 'where does it hurt?'…from then on, the whole relationship of signifier and signified, at every level of medical experience, is redistributed: between the symptoms that signify and the disease that is signified, between the description and what is described, between the event and what it prognosticates, between the lesion and the pain that it indicates. The clinic- constantly praised for its empiricism, the modesty of its attention, and the care with which it silently lets things surface to the observing gaze without disturbing them with discourse – owes its real importance to the fact that it is a reorganisation of depth, not only of medical discourse, but of the very possibility of discourse about disease.' (Foucault 1986a pxviii - xix)

Though this transformation opened up the possibility of the empirical study of disease, the consequence for modern health care is that the process of diagnosing and treating disease has become inherently excluding of the person. The doctor has gained a different and superior knowledge and therefore has power over the person who is sick, as do other health professionals such as nurses, clinical psychologists and psychotherapists. This is not a system that is exclusively about doctors and medicine.

David Armstrong (1995) explores Foucault's notion of 'space' or spatialisation in defining illness and identifies three levels at which it operates. The first is the process of cognitive mapping of the different elements of illness. This has come about by linking elements in 3 dimensions: symptom, sign and pathology. The second, the patient's body, became an object of study manifested in the clinical examination and post-mortem. The third process was the removal of the locus of health care from the patient's own home, to the 'neutral' space of the hospital or laboratory. These are the classic components of the 'medical model'. These three elements are linked during the empirical investigations that result in the 'diagnostic moment' (Rose 1994), that is, the moment when a diagnosis can be confirmed. An increasing number of complex technologies is used in order to orchestrate this as an event, for example the stethoscope, X-rays or scans. Not until the correct sequence of steps has been taken, or signs compiled, can the diagnosis be declared. The consequence of this for the patient, which is illustrated in Mike's story, is an agonising wait while the 'correct' sequence is assembled. Meanwhile Mike as a person is left suspended, knowing and not knowing his condition is serious.

Armstrong argues that the twentieth century has seen the rise of new forms of surveillance, such as public health. This has moved medicine into the realms of the 'normal' so that even the state of normal health has become problematised and requires monitoring (through screening programmes for example), and is defined through the notion of 'risk' of developing disease. Also, surveillance of psychosocial aspects of life such as anxiety, lifestyle, life history, chronic illness, and the concerns of the dying, has become a dimension of more progressive health care. The goal here is to normalise aberrant aspects. Those that do not conform to a notion of 'normal' are seen as requiring health care intervention.

As with the 'diagnostic moment' the dimension of time has its own, and different, currency in health care. Ronald Frankenberg (1988,1992) argues that health care as operated for example within a hospital, runs according to its own time (or perhaps this is simply the dimension of time associated with a particular disease as it runs its course from diagnosis to cure or death). He describes this phenomenon using the term 'anti-temporality', because it bears no relation to time in the 'real' world, and it is through operating in this time that power over the body is generated and status amongst the various parties that offer healing is made manifest. Within the hospital one is initiated into a new time dimension by admission procedures, through uniforms and white coats, through routines and rituals quite out of keeping with time outside. The day starts very early, sleep is interrupted, one's bodily functions are monitored and 'ordered' if not keeping 'proper' time. According to Frankenberg, the meaning of these rituals does not come from the necessity to heal disease, but is an act of conformity with biomedical practice. Likewise the course of a particular disease has its time defined through biomedical practices, from the 'diagnostic moment' to each stage where disease is declared as having worsened, is cured, or when it enters the stage of incurability, these moments are defined within a system of medical tests and investigations, within which declarations are made that define and categorise illness. Medical time operates according to an entirely different pattern of time from the one experienced by the person who is ill. Time for someone who is ill is suspended and frequently involves waiting for medical declarations to provide an explanation for their suffering.

These genealogies tell us that health care has progressively developed in such a way that it is inherently excluding of the person and sense of self. Investigation, categorisation and diagnosis of what become 'medical' problems require an objectified body, and not a person. Dealing with illness demands submission on the part of the person who is ill, and very possibly incarceration in an institution where disciplinary power is exerted over the individual until he or she is deemed sufficiently well to return to his or her life. This process mirrors what Talcott Parsons (1951) described as 'the sick role'. The Parsonian description refers to legitimate relinquishment of work and responsibility while one collaborates with medicine or health care practice in order to regain one's health. The Foucauldian perspective offers something equally necessary and assumed, but more sinister. It leaves one to question whether collusion with disciplinary power is necessarily positive or beneficial, and indeed whether alternatives to this exist.

However, to simply understand this 'absence' of self within health care as a product of biomedical dominance is inadequate. People, the lay public, often contribute willingly to the maintenance of medical suppression of 'self', as well as frequently challenging it, suggesting a relationship fraught with ambivalence (Lupton 1997). In looking for alternatives people adopt complementary therapies or lifestyle management strategies as a way of preventing or managing ill health: as they do this the influence of biomedicine enters further into daily life. This is not exclusively an issue in relation to mainstream health care. Many alternative therapies, it is argued, create an even more intense 'gaze' into individuals' lives than medicine. Lupton (1997) argues that these alternative understandings of the body are not more authentic, neither are they more liberating: they are simply different. But they do perhaps represent people's search for something more attentive to their sense of self.

Health and medical knowledge have themselves become commodities, taken up by the market and sold through the popular media as health products or health promoting regimes or lifestyles. According to Bunton (1997), health and its management have become dispersed and are no longer contained within the domain of health professionals and traditional health care institutions. This leaves individuals increasingly uncertain about their bodies; they therefore rely on expert knowledge but are also suspicious of it.

Thus, medicine and health care have developed in such a way that they have excluded the person, the sense of 'me'. The Foucauldian perspective does not see this as bad or wrong; indeed much of what has occurred has been liberating, and has made the scientific study of disease possible. As the body became conceptualised as a container for disease, and the object of legitimate study and manipulation in the name of managing disease, the idea of the person with a separate and individual identity also arose. The very possibility of a psychology of the self opened up, in need of acknowledgement and attention, to be nurtured and healed alongside the physical body. Paradoxically, this new separate identity of 'self', now appears to make medicine and health care incompatible in their current form with society and its need for care of the 'self'.

I have tried, here, to set out some of the reasons why biomedicine, and by this I mean all aspects of the dominant model of health care, not just the practice of doctors, has become such an important force within society. Also, why biomedicine, by its very nature, and the power structures by which it operates, is at the heart of why health care is experienced as unsatisfactory. What is important, is to acknowledge the power of biomedicine and health care, and how health and the desire for it have become deeply ingrained in contemporary culture, to the extent that 'health' has replaced to a great extent 'religion'. A huge market exists in supplying products to support this. It entails, in future, a continuing shift in focus away from formal health care, which is currently perceived as unsatisfactory, towards informal or commodified versions of 'health care'. Formal health care must urgently address and respond to this shift if it is to remain relevant in 21st century culture. Understanding health care's failure to attend to the sense of 'self' is key and is essential to renew the life of mainstream care.

'It is fatal to be a man or woman pure and simple; one must be woman-manly or man-womanly. It is fatal for a woman to lay the least stress on any grievance; to plead even with justice any cause; in any way to speak consciously as a woman. And fatal is no figure of speech; for anything written with that consciousness is doomed to death. It ceases to be fertilized. Brilliant and effective, powerful and masterly, as it may appear for a day of two, it must wither at nightfall; it cannot grow in the minds of others. Some collaboration has to take place in the mind between the woman and the man before the art of creation can be accomplished. Some marriage of opposites has to be consummated.' Virgina Woolf (1928, p102-3)

4. The Professions

Will gender continue to determine professional roles and working practices in health care?

While examining the role of the professions in health care, in particular the various roles adopted by the different health professions, it struck me that what we have created is a system whereby dealing with the sense of 'self' amongst those who are ill, is undervalued, often relegated to the work of an 'underclass'. The underclass, nurses, are defined in their work by their gender.

Virginia Woolf in her essay *A Room of One's Own*, written for the Arts Society at Newnham and Girton colleges, explores the theme of women and fiction. Her problem, having been asked to deliver a lecture on women and fiction, was that the subject had a fatal drawback; she would be unable to draw any conclusion or make any profound judgement on it. Instead, she explores both the absence and presence of women's writing, and simply states: 'with money and a room of one's own, that is funds to sustain writing and unencumbered space in which to work and think, we might come to know the place of women'. What strikes me about this masterly feminist essay is that one could substitute medicine or health care for fiction, nurses for women, and a similar picture would emerge.

Here I stray into very dangerous territory. I am not illuminating oppression of women. Much has been written about this, and much could still be written. Rather I am referring to gender as an active process: how organisations and organisational behaviour are socially constructed, determined through a 'gendering' process, not necessarily attached to the behaviours of men and women. These are more often reflected in polarisation of roles and functions, of what is valued and that which is unacknowledged. One aspect of this, as Davies (1995,1996) suggests, is to consider not only how women are excluded within organisational settings, but also the particular ways in which they are included:

'Provided, however, that we understand masculinity and femininity not as attributes of individuals but as cultural representations, provided we see the power and the privileging of masculinity and the construction of femininity not as separate and complementary but as something given a negative connotation as 'other' we can steer a path between some of the difficulties and begin to explore gendering of social institutions in a way that makes the dilemmas of caring, particularly the ambiguities and paradoxes of professional care much more explicit.' (Davies 1995, p23)

In health care, this process of 'genderisation' persists despite the fact that now 50% of doctors who qualify are women, and that a significant number of nurses are men.

Woolf fantasises about what would have happened if Shakespeare had an equally gifted sister called 'Judith'? What would she have produced? The answer, nothing. Without access to formal education (Shakespeare was educated at grammar school which was not open to girls), without the freedom to move to London, knock at the stage door, act a little, earn a little, help edit and improve plays before finding an outlet for his writing, and the motivation and desire to earn money for his family, none of his genius would have been realised. For Judith none of this would have been available. Woolf envisages Judith meeting an early death having run away from an arranged marriage to find her brother. She discovers all the doors shut, her only recourse the bed of a stage manager, and finding herself with child, she commits suicide.

Likewise for nurses. If nurses had access to a different set of resources how different would we find health care? Beyond Florence Nightingale we have to search hard for examples of nurses who are responsible for ground-breaking discoveries or who have had a powerful influence within the biomedical world. Why? The means to accomplish these achievements have not been provided. With low status, only partial access to an academic education, and barred therefore from accessing resources, knowledge or power within health care, nurses cannot make their mark. Since nurses do not themselves create the knowledge by which health care operates, becoming well versed or proficient within it is an act that demands significant mastery. Nursing is barely noticed, valued more in its absence (insufficient nurses to staff wards or ITU beds for example) than its presence. Here we have another problem within health care, an unequal balance amongst the various groups who deliver treatment and care. An absence of the range of influences that might represent the various caring parties or practices, and therefore offer balance or alternatives to health care as it is conventionally understood.

If, according to myth, the characters Tuke and Pinel liberated the insane through medically led progress, according to the Nightingale myth, the soldiers of the Crimea were liberated from their filthy, cold and otherwise deprived circumstances by unassuming feminine domesticity. Revisionist perspectives provide evidence that the Nightingale legacy, rather than challenging authority as her altercations with patriarchal medicine in the Crimea might suggest, reinforced submission to authority, and reproduced the hospital as a microcosm of society, class-bound and with strict divisions of labour determined by gender (Rafferty 1996). The more autonomous figure of the community nurse was devalued and largely ignored as proletarian, and because she was outwith the control of medicine.

The Nightingale vision for nurse training was to build moral character, rather than to educate, and reinforce gender and subordination as essential to professionalism in nursing. Subsequent attempts to reform nursing, in particular nurses' desire to achieve the status of an autonomous profession, have met with resistance, those with a progressive agenda invariably held back by the tensions inherent in the incompatibility of professionalising an intellectually subordinate group. According to Rafferty *'nursing as a female dominated occupation, does not fit easily into the traditional mould which the archetypal professions have been cast. Moreover, nursing itself is caught in a contradiction in so far as it provides the necessary support for medicine to maintain its dominance, thereby perpetuating the subordination of nursing to medicine.'* (p186)

Health care has developed as one of the purest examples of a system where work practices and hierarchy are determined rigidly by a gendered process. There is a patriarchal sexual division of work, medicine being masculine and nursing being feminine. According to Gamarnikov (1978) the division of labour between medicine and nursing that has mapped out the spheres of competence for each, was not based on an equal contribution to the healing process. Instead it created a stratified system of inter-professional inequality. Medicine claimed the sole right to define who becomes a patient. Nursing was relegated to a subordinate position, firstly, 'nursing the room' where sickness is housed, a role that encompasses assuring cleanliness and comfort, and secondly, assisting the doctor (a contemporary equivalent of this is the fact that a common responsibility of nurse executives in the health service is that of quality assurance). The nursing role resembles domestic labour, a proletarian function, and is at odds with nursing's recent claims to greater status and professionalisation.

Medicine looked to science to justify its position, and as science has been vested with the highly valued goals of progress and discovery, these have become dominant. Nursing on the other hand has struggled to define the sources of knowledge on which to base practice (Waerness 1992). Emergent resistance to the dominance of medicine led to a rejection of science by nurses. Instead they looked to the social and emotional sciences as sources of reference, at the same time as acting to support medical functions. The desire for distinctiveness leaves nursing ill defined, and is a source of ambivalence. Since knowledge about caring, the act of attending to a person's needs and identity, or 'self' as I will argue later, does not rest on the more dominant scientific paradigm, it does not as a result hold the status of an important and highly visible activity.

An important consequence of the gendered division of labour in health care has been the relative valuing, and attendant devaluing of certain tasks and functions. Science and treatment have been progressively given greater priority and accorded greater status than care. James (1989) likens the function of caring within health care to that of mothering, or emotional labour. The routine management of emotional life within the family is acknowledged only in its absence or when it goes wrong, as in the cases of delinquency or abandonment. Similarly in health care everyday caring functions are largely unnoticed except when the emotional demands of illness become intolerable and are manifested in medically defined psychological or physical pathology. Caring only becomes newsworthy when the need for caring is unmet. The professions as currently constructed contribute to the absence of care for people's 'selves', the very nature of professionalism creates advantage for those accorded status and power as a professional, and with it disadvantage for those who are not, heroic visibility, and at the same time, invisibility.

Doctors trained to use the scientific method are expected to absorb facts. They learn to understand that there is a diagnosis for every condition and a predefined course of treatment to deal with it. Little time or thought is devoted to the intricacies of human interaction or in critical reflection on medicine as an approach (Lupton 1994). There is a certainty about medical practice, judgements and decisions are made quickly and authoritatively, just enough time is allocated to the medical encounter to determine a course of action, such encounters are managed through overt and covert signals to patients. The signals maintain distance and prevent emotional upheaval or embarrassment. The boundaries between medical practice and the other health disciplines are rigidly maintained; nurses are not to stray into medical territory. The delineation of professional roles in health care is enshrined in legislation covering for example prescribing powers or professional registration. Roles are maintained by the everyday ways in which health care is organised. Nurses, however, find definitions of their practice elusive. They have not adopted concrete modes of understanding how their work makes a contribution.

Status and position in health care are reinforced in a myriad of ways. Frankenberg (1992) suggests that one mechanism is the manipulation of time. Time in health care is used to delineate status. Medicine requires exceedingly long training. The hospital consultant, a rarified being, is seen only at fleeting moments. In contrast junior doctors work around the clock, but because of this are indispensable. Nurses have their time rigidly controlled, their location at any point during the working day is known, as are their hours of work. They work their allotted time, their shift, and then leave work behind completely. Nurses are controlled by the clock, it is an inflexible system controlled by external forces; there is no room for individuality. Nurses are a collective, individual nurses are unknown:

'...even in a hospital like Beth Israel, nurses receive subtle lessons that reinforce the idea that they are inferior to doctors. These lessons in status are conveyed – either inadvertently or deliberately – in seating arrangements, body language, tone of voice, gesture, acknowledgement of effort, and lack of routine courtesy.

When I began observing nurses on Stoneman Four – the hospital's inpatient oncology unit – I was immediately struck by the implicit message of early morning rounds. Each day the three interns [or house doctors] assigned to the unit sat in front of the picture window that formed the cancer ward's back wall. Leaning against the left wall, the resident [or registrar] faced the interns (two men and one woman) and asked them to present their cases. Behind him stood a semicircle of nurses, who were also supposed to participate in the morning rounds.

But each morning, this huddle simultaneously included and excluded the nursing staff. The resident always kept his back to the nurses. He addressed the three interns, not the larger group. The nurses offered their insights about the condition of a particular patient, but always from the outfield. The resident never shifted his position to look at the nurses who were speaking. Their comments were heard, but he never invited them to move into the inner circle and become full members of the group.' (Suzanne Gordon 1998, p79)

May (1992) reveals how medical staff control dissemination of information about patients, often excluding nurses from such information, leaving them to acquire this from the patient directly. The difficulties this causes are compounded by the episodic encounters nurses have with patients even though both exist in the single geographical setting of the hospital ward. Nurses overcome this by getting to know patients more broadly and incorporating knowledge of their lives beyond the hospital into care routines. In this, nurses have created their own working practices and knowledge systems, and while these on the one hand extend yet further the territory of biomedical surveillance into emotional and social territories, they also represent a significant departure from medical practice in which patients themselves may control and participate.

If gender is a process as much as it is a physical matter, then health care is not static and will not necessarily remain in its current gendered form. There is some evidence to suggest that professional roles are evolving and responding to such broader social changes such as the feminisation of the workplace, and the need for nurses to take on aspects of medical practice to reduce the working hours of doctors. The way in which doctors and nurses relate to each other, negotiate their particular roles and working practices, has not been the focus of much research activity. This despite the fact that the dynamics of interprofessional working reflect the character of health care and have an important bearing on the quality of care.

In 1967 work by Leonard Stein in the United States drew attention to the ways in which the relationship between doctors and nurses was made to work, describing what he called 'the doctor-nurse game'. According to the rules of this game, the nurse needed at all costs to sustain good relations with doctors. Moments of disagreement over how to manage a particular patient had the greatest potential to threaten the relationship, especially when the nurse might have greater experience and feel the need to take a different course of action than that recommended by the doctor. Overt recommendations to the doctor over how to treat a patient would be unacceptable, and undermine the doctor's authority and omnipotence. Instead, nurses subtly disguised these so that information and advice could flow from the nurse to the doctor without this being apparent, and the doctor's position and authority were saved. The game may have maintained relations within safe limits, but open dialogue was absent.

Stein et al (1990) repeated the study twenty years later, and discovered that significant changes had taken place within American nursing. Advances in professional autonomy had taken place, shortages of nurses in certain specialities, and even the character of nursing was different. The movement towards autonomy, with nurses aspiring to work co-operatively as equal partners with other health professionals, doctors included, was probably an extension of the civil rights movement. The principal vehicles for the changes observed were, according to Stein and his colleagues, academic education and a growing militancy. Nurses, it appears, were no longer playing the game. Nursing education was socialising them to play according to different rules. They were observed to be 'stubborn rebels', their behaviour having an over-determined, even hostile quality. The doctors were left feeling confused. Nurses were basing their new practice on illness prevention, education and management of chronic illness within a holistic framework. The most positive outcome was a new, more interdependent relationship with medicine: *'when a subordinate becomes liberated, there is potential for the dominant one to be liberated too' (Stein et al 1990, p268).*

Nurses have for some time sought greater recognition of their professional status and have striven for greater autonomy. This, according to Davies (1996), is contradictory because both of these are essentially gendered experiences, and nurses ask for inclusion in a world already predicated on their present invisible inclusion. More important, the world of health care as currently constructed would not work without the inclusion of nurses in the conventional way. Bringing caring to the forefront of the present system, dominated as it is by medical science, would be impossible without damaging current conceptions of professional competence. Questions also remain about whether nurses can legitimately claim caring as nursing territory since medicine too is developing an emphasis on caring more broadly for people.

Pringle's (1998) study of women doctors in Britain and Australia suggests a complex and changing arena. The very presence of women in large numbers within the medical profession is transforming it. This is not as a result of some coherent, feminist movement, where women doctors are demanding and acquiring equal status and treatment. Rather it is simply through their presence. All the varieties of medical practice in which women find themselves are opening up possibilities for change and evolution.

One of the most interesting aspects of Pringle's study is its exploration of the particular impact of increasing numbers of women doctors on doctor – nurse relations. Women doctors appear to occupy an in-between position, the middle ground between doctors and nurses. At times they find it difficult to establish their status as doctors. They are frequently mistaken for nurses, and while they enjoy more collegiate relations with nursing staff, they can also be treated more harshly by nurses than their male counterparts. They seek to get on with nurses but also need to differentiate themselves from them. Women doctors are adopting some of the caring practices claimed by nurses, but feel quite threatened by nurses in advanced practitioner roles. It seems that in the evolving relations between women doctors and nurses one can observe the fluidity, the blurring of the boundary between medicine and nursing. This has also brought to the fore new difficulties. While subordination due to gender may be changing, a new distinction has emerged, that of 'class'. This can be observed in the freedom to choose how to dress and the greater independence enjoyed by women doctors. Nurses are unable to choose what they wear at work. Women doctors are perceived as being 'bright' while nurses are considered 'dumb'. Nursing may have gained professional autonomy, but may also be finding it increasingly difficult to maintain its monopoly over caring practice.

In a system constructed so crudely around gender, where overtly or inadvertently there is inequality, imbalance will be passed on and draw in other players, in particular patients. Organisational structures develop and reflect the gendered system (see for example Munby and Putman's (1992) discussion of bounded rationality). In its least negative form a polarisation occurs. Where there is also an overt hierarchy, this tends to be passed on. Doctors and nurses pass on the pecking order, nurses in their turn dominate. They impose their own powerlessness on to the people they care for. Nurses are not simply a subordinate group: like doctors they unknowingly pass on their subordinate status to patients. In health care this manifests itself in the rigidity in which people who are ill find their lives are managed and in the control they must relinquish.

Professionalism determined as an expression of stereotypical masculinity dictates particular forms of working. Time is a scarce commodity of high worth, withheld and only distributed where necessary. Knowledge has an elite and inaccessible quality, since it is so difficult to acquire it can not be easily passed on. Power relations are unequal and require a subordinate client, emotions are denied or suppressed as irrational. The professional edifice is maintained through invisible and unacknowledged support functions such as care assistants, domestic, clerical and portering staff. Likewise the care of 'self', the sense of 'me' amongst people who are ill, in a system defined by gendered male professionalism, is also relegated to the status of the invisible and the unimportant, and defined as the work of an underclass.

Given the profound oppositions and difficulties I have presented here, what solutions might there be? Virginia Woolf suggests two avenues. One solution might be to provide the substrate for change, to actively promote evolution, and in turn judge what might ensue. Like women writers, it might be possible to provide unencumbered space and the resources to use this space; to provide nurses, or other less dominant groups such as patients themselves, the means by which they may develop; to provide access to the highest echelons of academia, research, policy development, politics, and power (as is beginning to be explored through recent public and patient involvement initiatives); to actively promote the blurring of positions, authorities, knowledge and practice. New and different roles in health care will demand these changes. Through the blurring may evolve a new kind of professionalism, based on egalitarianism, the conscious harnessing of emotionality as opposed to an exclusive dependence on rationality, and interprofessional working practices. A greater priority may be given to caring practice and to the needs of people. This though, may risk an unpredictable outcome. Change may occur too slowly or too quickly, or occur through militancy, or fail because of resistance. The result might possibly be an unsatisfactory or unnecessarily bloody outcome. It may also preserve parallel hierarchies, forever at odds with one another.

An alternative may be to 'consummate a marriage of opposites', combine the various professions, create a single training, a single health profession; to merge and commingle the different practices; to place caring alongside science and treatment with the involvement of all engaged in health care; to recreate organisational structures to reflect this revolution. The danger here would be to risk that which is currently invisible, because of the over-riding dominance of what is already highly visible.

Either way, a new professionalism is needed: one that has not derived from gender.

'The hospital, the modern cathedral, lords it over this hieratic environment of health devotees. From Stockholm to Wichita the towers of the medical centre impress on the landscape the promise of a conspicuous final embrace. For rich and poor, it is turned into a pilgrimage through check-ups and clinics, back to the ward where it started.' (Illich, 1976 p87).

5. Architectures of Treatment

Does the built environment of health care contribute to the impersonal and controlling atmosphere?

Architects and architecture have frequently been the focus of debate. Often there are bitter feuds and much comment on, and criticism of, new buildings, on everything from the buildings for large corporations or galleries, to supermarkets. Comment largely surrounds the aesthetics of a building or development. Whilst architecture is not in the main considered an art form, and it is felt to be quite distinct from sculpture or painting, the look of a building attracts interest. Buildings are observed to be either in sympathy with traditional architectural styles, or a radical departure. They merge with the immediate environment or confront it. The authors of these buildings, architects, become in turn enormously powerful, respected members of society, the arbiters of all that is aesthetic. Alternatively, they are outcast for the denigration imposed by their buildings on the form of our urban horizon. The National Gallery, Canary Wharf, the British Library, the Millennium Dome, Tate Modern, all have attracted much comment. Buildings attract attention.

According to Neil Leach (1997) debate surrounding architecture has largely been in relation to form. Little attention has been paid to semantics, or how a building may be read, or how one might understand its content. Architecture needs to move beyond simplistic Pevsner-like stylistic categorisation. Little attention is given to buildings as physical manifestations of society or social order, to the way they encode the hierarchies and interconnections of society in their external and internal forms. There is a connection between a building's purpose and the way the building reflects and contributes to this purpose. Buildings do not simply reflect the function they were designed to house, they also create it.

Leach draws together writings from many of those most influential in twentieth century Western thought to demonstrate how they have written about architecture, or used it as a metaphor in their explorations of society and social order. Within these writings, buildings are powerful forms of expression. For example the museum and slaughterhouse are in turn represented by Georges Bataille as expressions of society. In France the museum, the first type of building to house public collections of art, was established in Paris directly following the storming of the Bastille, and was therefore founded on bloody revolution to house trophies. The museum is mischievously described by Bataille as 'the colossal mirror in which man finally contemplates himself in every respect, finds himself literally admirable, and abandons himself to the ecstasy expressed in all the art reviews'. In contrast, the slaughterhouse, also founded on blood, since it emerged from a place for the ritual killing of animals for religious purposes, is no longer a place of ritual public celebration. It is rejected and hidden, quarantined, to allow people to bear what Bataille suggests is a reflection of their own ugliness.

Siegfried Kracauer explores how space within buildings is used to both create and represent particular aspects of social order. The hotel lobby is compared with the church or cathedral. In the latter, those congregating in the space within the building become a community, united in their reality to find common purpose in existence. The occupants of the hotel lobby are there not to be with others, not to enter into a community: their purpose is to remain anonymous. The hotel lobby's only purpose is to encompass those within it, to maintain detachment from daily life. It displaces people from daily hustle and bustle into a kind of void. Further, Kracauer examines the way space is used within employment agencies to represent and reinforce images of the community within. The production process and vagaries of market forces dominate the internal ethos. The environment is structured around purposeless waiting, created as a demoralising, meaningless activity. Waiting within the building has been devised as a form of production, a manifestation of capitalism.

Other writers have considered the effect architecture has beyond individual buildings or archetypes. Barthes for example considers urban semiology. The city is seen as a language that cannot be represented in maps or plans. Buildings have meaning, the way they are constructed, and are organised into streets and areas, they are signifiers. A neighbourhood has a life and meaning beyond its objective geography:

'the city is a discourse and this discourse is truly a language, we speak our city, the city where we are, simply by living in it, by wandering through it, by looking at it' (Barthes 1986/1998 p168).

Similarly, planners who use representational models or simulations to find ways to create order and thereby meet modern needs for transportation find, for example in Rome, a permanent conflict between the need for modern planning and the 'semantic charge given to the city by its history'.

Architecture according to Ameri (1998) adopts designs for buildings according to their function through assuming and adopting cultural norms. For example a house designed to provide for the function of 'sleeping', also inherently adopts cultural ideals such as those surrounding 'proper' sexual norms. Sleeping areas are, for example, separated into individual bedrooms. Likewise all of architectural practice inevitably incorporates the cultural systems upon which the building's particular function is based.

Using the example of the library, Ameri traces how space has been used in library design from medieval times to the present, and how it reflects the way that writing as a precarious or pernicious representation of speech or reality has variously been viewed. In early libraries books were kept in locked cupboards, or somewhat later were chained to shelves. Renaissance libraries were designed to give a sense of transition to the world of books. There were grand entrances, vestibules and staircases; the books were separated from the ground on galleries and corridors. Modern libraries are designed around three spaces: circulation space, reading space, and book stacks. Books are stacked on top of each other in central space, and while they may easily be removed from the library, books retain their identity within the library through elaborate catalogues and codes whereby the book may be easily replaced on its return. In each library form, Ameri argues, books are in place and under control: *'this common aim reflects in no small measure, the ambivalence of Western culture toward the representation that the library seeks to **place** [author's emphasis] and keep in place: writing' (p295).*

In contrast to writing, art is not considered an approximation of the 'real' world; the art museum therefore is characterised by designs that transport one from the every day world to a world in parallel. Galleries are frequently sited away from or on a hill above and separated from the city, they have elaborate entryways that one must pass through to enter the world of art. Ameri argues that these building types condition how we conceive modes of representation such as writing or art, and through buildings the 'real' world that art and writing are intended to represent is placed in opposition to them. To this extent architecture has a subversive affect, undermining the authenticity of art and writing as reflections of, or accurate records of, reality.

If there are powerful representations of society and social order in building archetypes and in the language of cities, what is manifested in the architecture of health care? How are hospital buildings, clinics, nursing homes, primary care centres, doctors' surgeries, operating theatres, and hospital complexes to be read? How does the built environment of health care reflect its social order? Are its hierarchies encoded in its buildings and how does it reflect the powerful discourses already described? Is it possible to see a parallel perpetuation to that set out earlier, of the absence of 'self', or the sense of 'me' in its architecture?

Relatively little critical exploration of the influence of architecture on health care exists. Foucault has arguably written most persuasively on the theme of institutional architecture, and is strongly of the opinion that this architecture both reflects and promotes the system within it. In prisons, asylums and hospitals the buildings reflect, promote and reinforce surveillance, disciplinary power and correction, Bentham's Panopticon is the architectural form of these processes:

'at the periphery an annular building; at the centre, a tower; this tower is pierced with wide windows that open onto the inner side of the ring; the periphetic building is divided into cells, each of which extends the whole width of the building; they have two windows, one on the inside, corresponding to the windows of the tower; the other, on the outside, allows the light to cross the cell from one end to the other. All that is needed, then is to place a supervisor in the central tower and to shut up in each cell a madman, a patient, a condemned man, a worker or a schoolboy… The panoptic mechanism arranges spatial unities that make it possible to see constantly and to recognise immediately. In short, it reverses the principle of the dungeon; or rather of its three functions – to enclose, to deprive of light and to hide – it preserves only the first and eliminates the other two. Full lighting and the eye of a supervisor capture better than darkness, which ultimately protected. Visibility is a trap.' (Foucault 1977 p200)

The Panopticon created an efficient model or machine for incorporating into buildings the very mechanics of power and discipline. It made it possible to continuously observe occupants without being observed, and rendered those who observe anonymous. The director could oversee staff so that the observers themselves could also be observed. Each cell was the setting for continuous monitoring of its incumbent and therefore the outcome of the corrective process. In buildings designed according to the model of the Panopticon fewer staff were needed to supervise a greater number of occupants. Victorian mental asylums, until recently the setting for much of mental health care in this country, are built in close sympathy with the Panopticist ideal.

Few buildings within health care could be said to adhere strictly to Bentham's design. However, the principles of panopticism are contained within forms of building, and physical structures are the basis for many institutional power systems. Surveillance is inherent in many institutional health care settings.

Lyndsay Prior (1988) suggests that hospital plans are archeological records. The study of elements of hospital design reveals changes in the objects of medical attention and in how disease and illness are conceptualised. Prior explores changes in the design of children's wards over the years, and changes in asylum architecture between 1807-1845 and the psychiatric units built between 1972-1982. Hospital designs are revised from time to time; architecture is observed to both define and reflect the object of therapy. Prior focuses on the hospital ward for his observations. He notes that hospital architecture is capable of many and varied forms of expression. In each setting 'the hospital bed' plays a most important role, and represents the locus for medical and nursing observation. The pavillion hospital and the Nightingale ward were influenced by miasmic theory: space between beds and the ability for air to circulate were felt to be important to contain disease. As germ theory became established, the Nightingale design was fragmented and the spaces between beds were divided by glass partitions.

The development of children's wards reflects the emerging theories of child development. In early design an authoritarian atmosphere dominates. Later, from the 1960s, space is set aside for the observation of children during 'natural' activity. Later still, continuity of parental contact is accommodated. In psychiatric facilities there is a less obvious or at times absent association between theories about therapeutic practice in relation to mental illness and architecture. Most psychiatric facilities are disciplinary and authoritarian rather than therapeutic in design.

Prior identifies three features of how space is organised architecturally in hospitals. Firstly, rather than the cell or cubicle, the bed is the dominant spatial unit. This serves two functions: it emphasises and identifies individuals, and provides a means to control the occupant. Facilities are organised to regulate and demarcate bodily functions. Emphasis is given in design plans to toilets, bathrooms and treatment rooms. Within the facility, office space is allocated according to hierarchies. The higher one is within the hierarchy, the larger one's space. Post-1982 psychiatric unit architecture much more clearly expresses its focus on the continuity of care with the community. More emphasis is placed on social interaction as an important component of therapy. Prior suggests that these developments may represent a movement away from a panoptic model.

More recently there has been a large scale dismantling of in-patient psychiatric facilities, including many Victorian buildings, following government policy for care in the community. Contrary to the idea that this is progressive and welcomed, debate continues about how appropriate it is to construct a model of care around a virtual or 'bed-less' community support model. Issues of public safety have been exploited to demand a return to secure facilities for the most seriously ill or disturbed. There has also been a suspicion that change was driven by economic considerations more than by a genuine commitment to a new form of mental health care. This may be true, but it may also reflect the central place structures of containment have in public consciousness. Prior's analysis perhaps too readily assumes that evolving hospital design necessarily marks a fundamental move away from the structures that encode and reinforce panopticism.

The Nuffield Trust's own authoritative survey of *50 Years of Ideas in Health Care Buildings* (Francis et al 1999) reveals an ongoing emphasis on enhancement of workflow, functionalism, standardisation and cost-containment in NHS hospital design. For example the most efficient consulting rooms for specialist doctors were found to be those where each doctor worked with two rooms, an examination room and a consultation room where a patient's notes could be recorded. The examination room had a separate door by which patients could enter and exit without disturbing the doctor. Hospital wards were designed following detailed observations of nurses' walking patterns between bed and treatment areas. Little or no thought was given to how these buildings are experienced by patients, their meaning for the people who use them, or the effects of hospital design on quality of life or recovery. From the 1970s onwards cycles of economic and political crisis have severely restricted any investment in creative or theoretical approaches to planning and development. Although there is some interest in the design of health care buildings that support and reflect patient-centred care, there exists no research or evaluation programme into NHS hospital design.

Jonathon Hughes (1997) explores the interrelationship between town planning and hospital design. Concepts of the body and disease, manifested in a preoccupation with circulation, efficiency and health (a corporeal analogy), can be seen in modernist urbanism and in parallel models of hospital design. Town-planning adopts 'clinical' approaches to sanitising, separating and creating specialisation within areas of the city, the main goal being to optimise traffic flow. These approaches bear a remarkable similarity, for example, to Friesen's ' circulatory logic for the modern hospital' or the so-called 'race track' ward design.

Within hospitals the 'custodial' model of care gave way to a model that promoted mobility, for example post-surgery. This then required wards to be designed so that supervision and surveillance of patients remained possible through staff stations, electronic monitoring devices and communication systems. In hospital design as a whole, movement or circulation within the hospital was promoted, while at the same time patients and their modes of treatment became increasingly specialised and categorised. Each department catered for different types of patients (for example the intensive care unit) or for different procedures or investigations. Patients then needed to be able to move between the various departments with ease.

There appears for Hughes to be an obsessive preoccupation with order, efficiency and correctitude within hospital design, indicative of a deep anxiety about the underlying uncontrollability of disease and death. It may be that the commitment to functionalism and efficiency is an attempt to develop a 'curative architecture' – a flawed project since it only serves as a form of denial, an attempt to cover over medical impotence in the face of human frailty. Recent hospital design, then, may have let go of some of the past, but has retained its tendency for regulation and segregation: *'illness remains as prevalent as ever, ever testing both the medical profession's curative skills and the modern hospital's ability to adapt in response. Modern architecture has sought to cope with such problems and offer understanding and solutions whilst constantly threatened with change. But the apparent futility of such a constant heroic struggle suggests an alternative view, proposing modernist hospital architecture as one of denial, obsessively seeking to defeat the challenges thrown at it through the valiant declamation of its own efficiency and ability to cope, all vouchsafed by its supposedly scientific validity.' (p285)*

Just as libraries were designed around the idea of writing, there appear to be some persistent themes surrounding how the physical environment of health care has been constructed. The early utilitarian vision has been maintained and reinforced, creating a kind of entrapment of the person who is in need of care. This is most apparent in the way patients are maintained and retained within the hospital building until they are 'discharged' back to their lives and communities, presumably 'well'. Retention is most commonly achieved through the hospital bed, a now carefully managed commodity. Individuals are placed in an identifiable, fixed space, within which treatment can be delivered and the ministrations of nurses and doctors focused. Data on progress can easily be collected. Hospitals therefore represent productivity not sanctuary.

The hospital bed seems to be predicated much more around power and control, than the need for rest or recuperation. Indeed in many instances, lying in bed is believed to be counter-therapeutic. The only alternative to this is driven by fast throughput, production style processes reinforced by policies of efficiency and cost-control: day case treatment settings often replace beds with trolleys. The locus of control is maintained, this time on a wheeled conveyor belt. The comfort level is reduced like it is in McDonalds, to speed post-operative arousal and thereby early departure.

The clinical setting adopts, through its architectural presence, both the interior design and building structure, a message of progress, cleanliness and efficiency. This takes precedence over comfort, reassurance, information, or participation. The architecture supports the quite literal transportation of people into the world of treatment and its time dimensions. Hospitals, clinics and surgeries are made up of dormitories, waiting areas and the settings for confrontation with medicine. There is a process of separating people from normal life in the manner with which they are conducted from the hospital door to wards or departments inside. Through checking-in procedures one is located and monitored by computer; waiting areas like Kracauer's employment agencies are designed to keep one in limbo until moved further within, and also act as a reminder about who is in control. Factory-like clinic designs give false reassurance about progress through the appointment system. Clinic, ward and consultation room structures reinforce the separation between patient and professional. Little effort is put into aesthetics. With few exceptions these recreate and promote the images and processes of health care. Segregation, surveillance, and control predominate, and individual identity is negated. These are the architectures of treatment and not of personal care.

Policy makers for health care need to determine the form for future buildings. Buildings, whether they are large hospitals or local surgeries, need to be different. They need to embody different meanings. In particular buildings need to convey recognition of people's sense of self, of 'me', rather than promote, as they do now, the collective need for health care to get 'the job done' by controlling and processing patients. In doing so they need to consider how our health care institutions can be designed to represent and create structures that relinquish dominating and ordering forms, and instead use architecture to portray and promote partnership and personal attention. They need to convey the sense that I matter, that the way I experience this encounter with health care is as important as its outcome, they need to be places where I can feel at home rather than transported, powerless into an alien environment over which I have no control. Critically, buildings need to foster self-action by people in relation to their health since increasingly this will be demanded by future generations of health care users who may be much more reluctant to relinquish themselves unquestioningly to biomedicine.

'As knowledge expands, many people will grow more knowledgeable, and the public more highly educated, but it does not follow that they will either claim or bow to the power of the expert. The curious paradox of the future will then be that technological growth generates its demystification, and consequently undermines its own supremacy.' (Haug 1973 p209)

6. 'Me'

Is a new value system needed for health care – devised to foster people's sense of self, while also attending to their health?

Thus far I have attempted, in what are perhaps a collection of loosely connected themes, to reveal how health care represented by its physical structures, its architecture, interior design, and ambience, undervalues or sets aside the relationship between health care and the people who make use of it. This occurs through the people who make up the professions providing treatment and care, and also through the system by which people's bodies are understood, treated and cared for.

It is not necessarily intentional, but is manifested in the ways in which health care has evolved and established common practices, knowledge systems and authorities, its architecture as well as its workforce.

Most of the writers who have influenced me are not tempted in the main into 'revisioning'; dreaming or fantasising a future where some of the more negative consequences of what health care has become are undone, nor do they offer alternatives. Rather, they see inherent problems within present structures, and see the task of understanding these as sufficient, a task which itself can bring about change. In any case, the biomedical knowledge and practice that underpin health care are deeply ingrained in and, to some extent, determine our very culture, our social relations and our understanding of our bodies. It is not a system that can in any straightforward way be overthrown, reformed or refashioned. This is perhaps why the many attempts at health care reform simply have reinvented the very problems they sought to solve: they reappear in a slightly different form or place. It may be that no unifying model or solution to the problems of health care is waiting to be discovered.

Throughout, I have used 'me' synonymously with the sense of 'self'; I refer to those aspects of us that define who we are. Our self is also represented by the particular things that we want or need to maintain a sense of self intact in relation to our life, to our biography. Here immediately one can see in the stories of Mike and Simon, presented earlier, that health care is not currently organised to preserve and attend to the need to maintain intact 'selves'. Indeed health care serves in general to remove or negate this, as I have already outlined. It is not a system created to preserve and value individuality or autonomy since there is already a single, dominant value system – biomedicine, and the discourse of one's 'self' is unlikely to coincide with this system. The very notion on which biomedicine rests runs counter to individualism and autonomy since biomedicine largely deals with the science of the collective, rather than the individual, measuring performance and developing understanding of disease through populations, norms and averages. Correspondingly there is a commonly held lay belief that in order to return to health from ill-health, one should relinquish control over oneself and put oneself into the hands of the experts. This is a particularly strongly, although not universally, held desire in situations of acute or life threatening illness.

The notion that one may relinquish 'self' to another, raises a second issue in relation to 'self', that is, generally care of 'self' is a matter for 'oneself'. Despite this, health care has traditionally removed or taken over responsibility for care of 'self' as an act of benevolence, often even when a person is able to, or at least partially able; to manage this for themselves. Once this function is taken over there is resistance to relinquishing it, to passing care of 'self' back again, and to promoting the re-establishment of 'self' care as a legitimate object of health care. Mutual involvement or partnership in the management of 'self' care is not an obvious feature of care or treatment systems.

Care of the 'self' is more than those acts in which one maintains oneself practically, more than feeding, dressing or washing oneself, or maintaining one's immediate environment through housework or employment. The act of 'self' care goes deeper than this; it is an intrinsic part of life, a valued and systemised activity that may take on different forms depending on one's culture or beliefs (Foucault 1986). Care of the 'self' is more than simply keeping oneself healthy, or adopting a healthy lifestyle; it is also the activity of 'cultivating oneself', and is composed of a whole set of occupations or 'technologies', including cultivating self knowledge and educating oneself, also acquiring knowledge of activities that involve risk. The recommendations of a doctor with regard to keeping oneself healthy are only one set of activities that may be adopted or rejected; acquiring the knowledge to be one's own 'health counsellor' is important to adopting 'health practice' in a framework for everyday life (Foucault 1986). While these practices may share many common features amongst people they are also individual and particular, and are largely distinct from any medically prescribed regime. According to Foucault (1984) one of the features of modern times is that we are seeing a re-affirmation of the autonomy of the 'self', and therefore the ways in which we are enabled to care for ourselves by health care may become increasingly important. Indeed it is the modern conception of the body and disease that is making possible the continuation of practices of self care:

At a time when we have lost faith in the sanctity of moral codes, have no wish to be bound by legal imperatives and are forced to rationalise our fate in terms of our choices, the new ontology of ourselves constituted by medicine appears to offer us a rational, secular and corporeal solution to the problem of how we should lead our lives for the best; of how we might make the best of our life by adjusting it to our truth, by letting medicine enlighten our decisions as to how to live it.' (Rose 1994, p69)

Thus, health and health care are likely to become increasingly important in the coming decades. Medicine as defined by Rose, however, is more than medical practitioners or the health service. It is also the more generalised commodified form of medicine, such as writing about what is healthy in books, newspapers and magazines, and the products sold to help us stay healthy in health food shops, chemists and supermarkets.

In the context of health care, care of 'self' can be seen in two ways. Firstly, there is what I shall refer to as self-care, that is the activities one adopts in order to keep well, prevent disease or manage illness and its effects if illness arises. This notion of care of the 'self' is in keeping with a number of current health movements such as health promotion and self-care programmes, and client-centred care initiatives. These however have been rather limited and narrow in their outlook since the focus is largely on disease prevention, physical self-care and managing illness or disability. Self-care is only part of what I shall refer to as 'self' care. 'Self' care is broader, it encompasses all that is required to take care of one's identity, and how one cultivates as well as nurtures and sustains one's 'self', and is a feature of late modern society (Giddens 1991). Health care tends to dominate and direct self-care but from its own single vantage point (in general through a process of instruction such as in health education messages or the advice a doctor may give about managing a particular health problem). However, it also neglects or fails to acknowledge the need to care for people's 'selves', even among its own staff members who suffer high levels of stress as a result of the pressures of their work (Williams et al 1998). While self-care is important and could be given much greater status as I shall argue, it is the wider 'self' care that I believe needs to be incorporated into health care in a way that is not done currently.

Health care refashioned so that care of 'self' is central, would make a genuine commitment to helping individuals develop their own self-care practices to prevent disease or manage illness. At the same time health care would offer greater accommodation in treatment and care settings of the way individuals cultivate their 'selves', for example by incorporating the particular ways in which individuals express their identity, manage stress, organise daily life; how they maintain a sense of being valued by others. These are all relevant to individual health, episodes of ill health and the process of recovery. Health care could enable individuals to have greater autonomy in relation to their health and to illness. At the same time health care could ensure that where illness requires treatment or care, personal beliefs and practices that are about care of 'self', or maintaining a sense of one's personal identity and of being valued by others, are accommodated. This is a highly complex shift in orientation to achieve since currently health care is conceived almost exclusively around dependence on health care professionals and a system that prioritises efficiency and orderliness over catering for highly personal needs.

Two parallel changes are needed: firstly, promote greater autonomy for people while using health care to assist them to manage their health themselves, where this is appropriate; secondly, create caring environments that make care for people's 'selves' a priority. Acknowledgement and support for self-action in relation to one's health is a necessary pre-requisite to regaining the sense of 'self', of 'me', in health care since the absence of this is at the core of depersonalising experiences. If self-action were felt to be automatic rather than unusual, then the structures and relationships within health care would evolve accordingly. Without this it may not be possible to create the environments that value people's 'selves'.

Social changes are occurring that will create momentum for change in health care. One of the barriers to greater autonomy for people to manage their health is that access to health information and products is largely under the control of doctors. While there may be resistance to change from doctors and other health professionals, this control is in the process of being undermined through growing distrust in the medical profession, and a vast parallel market in health care commodities and information that will expand further with the internet. The idea of the medical practitioner as arbiter of health care product consumption is in the process of undergoing significant erosion. Yet medical expertise is important for people when trying to determine what may be needed for a particular health problem. The products and advice that should be under the control of medical expertise, and the assumption that medical control is always necessary, is being questioned. One example where health care structures could be questioned is the prescription. This is the focus of the majority of medical encounters, but it could be argued places too much control in the hands of the doctor. To date control has been seen as a necessity for reasons of safety, preventing drug abuse and ensuring optimal treatment for any given condition. A consequence of the doctor's role has been the development of a prescription dependent culture in which consumers are dissatisfied if they leave the surgery without a prescription, and doctors who reach too readily for pharmaceutical solutions to people's problems.

What needs to be determined is how many health or illness related commodities such as pharmaceutical products, technical aids and diagnostic tests need to remain within the formal structures of health care, and how many might be allowed to become accessible through carefully regulated market based systems. Also, what would the consequences of this be, particularly to those at risk of being excluded from the best health and self-care practices through poverty or disadvantage? To what extent could a commodified, but openly accessible system, be devised and how might this be utilised by formal health care to enhance its current activities? How might greater autonomy in accessing health products and in making decisions about their health change the relationship people have with their doctors?

Studies indicate that the relationship between self-care initiatives and attendant reductions in uptake of formal health care is not straightforward. Self-care programmes have been established as a means of managing excessive demand for health care, especially demand that is unnecessary or inappropriate. It has been estimated that 25 % of visits to primary care physicians are unnecessary especially since almost all minor acute ailments can be managed through self-treatment (see Steinweg et al 1998), and that these visits may be reduced by between 7 and 17 % by providing self-care guidance. Self-care programmes are designed to optimise and enhance people's ability to confidently manage these health problems. One such programme (Steinweg et al 1998) whereby family members were given brief instruction on self-care and a 'take care of yourself' manual that, in the event of illness, could be used with a health promotion pharmacist to select one of a range of 45 non-prescription medications. The programme resulted in an average reduction of 4 clinic visits per family per year. However, other studies suggest that these programmes may privilege certain groups, for example the better educated and those from higher income groups, or people with young families who are high users of services in any case. Those who are less advantaged have been found to access formal health care more often and are less likely to receive care from a specialist once a problem has been defined as requiring formal care (Alberts et al 1998).

The consumers of health-related products represent a major market. A large industry exists around both health-related products and media driven health-related advice: these fall into two main categories. The first is products or advice designed to enhance or promote good health and the maintenance of health, such as vitamin supplements or complementary therapies and information leaflets. The second category includes products designed to treat or relieve health-related problems; these are largely for minor, self-limiting conditions, and include an array of non-orthodox or complementary therapies.

According to Srnka and Portner (1997) an important component of the health products market is a growing emphasis on self-care. This may include for example exercise regimes, home pregnancy testing, nutritional supplements and self-medication with non-prescription drugs, and is likely to expand vastly in the future as new products are developed and marketed. Through this market, self-care is increasingly used as an effective alternative to medical care. The term self-care in this context refers to individuals who act on their own behalf to manage their own well-being or illness, without resorting to the health care system. The discovery of 'self' here is likened to a revolution: 'probably the most significant event in health care since the discovery of germ theory of disease is the discovery of the 'self' (Levin cited by Srnka and Porter).

Self-care, it is suggested, portends a move away from professionally constructed health care to lay or social control. Recognition of the limitations of professional care and a growing distrust of professionals have led to a belief in one's own ability to take control of one's health or to compensate for the inadequacies of professional care. There is also a parallel demand for products that increase one's capacity for self-care such as health information, home laboratory tests, medical devices and non-prescription products. Alongside this has been an explosion in the use of alternative and complementary therapies, either used instead of or in parallel with conventional health care.

This growing industry has yet to be harnessed in any co-ordinated way so that it may be seen as an integral and valued part of health care. The market could be opened up and constrained less by regulation or the closed-shop nature of how formal health care is currently organised. This market could be exploited and enhanced for the benefit of consumers, since demand for health-related products would suggest they desire this, or for its potential to ease the burden on over-stretched services. In the United States pharmacists have been recognised as playing a key role in providing and supporting self-care. This role has been facilitated by changes in legislation; in many states pharmacists can administer treatments such as immunisations, or run health maintenance programmes such as weight loss clinics in addition to fulfilling their statutory duties to provide advice regarding medications. Pharmacists who run self-care or self-medication programmes do so through consultations conducted in an area separate to but within the pharmacy; a charge is made for their time and for any products bought as a result. The consultation is recorded and people attending are advised if it is important that they see a doctor. Since pharmacies are open long hours and often 7 days per week, they have the potential to become a very accessible and effective form of health care (Srnka and Portner 1997).

In the UK the relationship of pharmacies to formal health care is close, particularly the relationship with general practitioners. A much closer alliance would enable pharmacies to assist with a much wider range of self-care activities. Investment could be made to enable pharmacists to develop much greater responsibility for facilitating self-management within a system that provided information and support for self-care, but also assisting entry into formal health care through a close relationship with primary care.

The internet is making access to health advice, consultations, drugs, even those that require a doctor's prescription, readily available through electronic means. NHS Direct and NHS Online are early examples of how the health service may provide health information targeted at self-management. The structures to support self-care are developing already as a result of consumer demand; enhancing these and creating an interface with formal health care would be possible but needs central co-ordination. The effects of the internet on existing care systems such as pharmacies and primary care have yet to be seen and may have the effect of altering use and expectations of these resources dramatically.

People who attend for professional care will increasingly do this as an active choice rather than the only choice. The relationship with health professionals needs to unfold accordingly, to value people's desire for self-care, and recognise as well the fact that each individual has their own particular version of self-care practices that may not accord closely with professionally determined biomedical versions.

Health, illness, birth and death form the most significant events shaping one's biography, and these largely occur within health care settings. Health professionals could assume a new role in assisting individuals construct their own life narratives in relation to events such as birth, illness and death, whereby individuals seek ways of making sense of themselves in relation to their life and their social world by talking about their experiences. This could could replace activities currently under the control of doctors that people could do for themselves. It is likely that multiple understandings of health, illness, disease and methods of managing each will emerge as lay belief systems become more prominent: biomedicine will increasingly provide only one source of knowledge among many. How those steeped in the traditions of biomedicine will adapt to this new determination to adopt self-care is uncertain and will require preparation and openness to individuals and their particular version of 'self' care. One can envisage that the boundaries of formal care will change. A much more fluid territory may emerge, where people at times make informed and relevant choices without accessing formal care, and at other times use formal care as a source of advice and help about how to act in relation to their health.

Self-management has to date been taken up as a means of controlling health care demand in order to reduce health care costs. While this may be an important incentive for change in health care, reduced demand does not follow as a matter of course. Also, restricting developments to self-management initiatives does not reflect a deeper understanding of what a shift to accommodating 'self' within health care actually entails. Being enabled to act for oneself in relation to one's health is at the core of a wider need, that is to feel that one's 'self' is genuinely valued and taken into account within health care settings.

Christiana Miewald (1997) suggests that caution should be exercised in relation to self-care, because many of the themes of self-care, for example individualism, self-control and autonomy, are basic social themes for the white, middle classes. Reinforcing the dominance of these themes also tends to privilege the groups for whom they seem natural or culturally familiar. Formal health care services are settings which espouse the health beliefs and practices dominant within white middle class culture; 'whiteness' is privileged through the construction of knowledge systems and cultural practices that are presumed to be 'normal'. In contrast, ethnic or other subordinated communities are settings where alternative cultural meanings are generated and maintained. Here when illness is experienced, decisions are made about whether to comply with or resist the recommendations of formal dominant health care.

Miewald evaluates the impact of an American community and health awareness and monitoring clinic that was established to occupy an intermediary location between formal health care and communities, and to be less dominated by the culture and practices of biomedicine. The role of the clinic programme was to facilitate self-management of chronic illnesses such as diabetes and hypertension to occupy a kind of 'deterritorialised' space in the hope of addressing issues such as poverty, segregation and health.

The clinic was seen to both succeed and fail. It succeeded in providing a different, supportive and less formal health care setting. Where it failed was in its adoption of an empowerment model based on advice on diet and lifestyle derived from white, middle class conceptions of 'healthy living', without addressing issues of poverty, culture and segregation that make conformity difficult for people. Failure to conform was experienced as a source of guilt, when in reality participants did not have the means to conform. Miewald suggests that what is needed is the ability to move beyond the lifestyle focus of chronic disease self-care and instead affirm differences in cultural expression and recognise and challenge the causes of ill health. Instead of traditional health education, what is needed is to listen to the voices and concerns of people who become excluded from the realms of biomedical practice, and create non-dominating forms of health care. In the community and health awareness clinic, where clients resisted the advice of health professionals and refused to comply, this served a positive purpose, in that staff were forced to devise evermore patient centred approaches. As Miewald states

'While [the clinic] does not entirely do away with many of the dominative aspects of biomedicine, it does provide a unique, border space in which people are free to construct their versions of self-care and at the same time feel secure in knowing that they are receiving monitoring and care. It is within the tension between biomedicine and the community, at the intersection of different ways of knowing that the possibility exists for the hybridisation of health care'. (p361)

Less dominating forms of health care are needed much more widely, and not only to overcome the particular problems of including ethnic and marginalised groups within mainstream health care. Models of client centred care have been adopted in a variety of health care settings, the goal being to overcome the inequality intrinsic to the doctor-patient relationship. For example, when medication is prescribed, most frequently an appropriate medicine for a particular condition is entirely determined by the medical practitioner with little reference to the person it is designed to treat, other than some rather cursory advice about how and when to take it. If the person then fails to take the medication this is deemed to be 'non-compliance'. Models of care have been devised and evaluated whereby there is an involvement of the person in determining what should be the favoured treatment, and in monitoring the effects of the medication and any changes that might be needed subsequently (Chewning and Sleath 1996). However, even in these more enlightened approaches, health professionals view people's care of themselves as supplemental to professional care, even though, with respect to prescribed medication, people are entirely responsible for deciding whether or not they use the medication. Health care is the supplemental care; not people's care of themselves (Dean 1995).

Health care has sought to find ways to facilitate self-care, but policies designed to promote self-care could not as yet be constituted as a co-ordinated movement. There has been no concerted attempt to grasp what providing for individuals in this way might mean, or what a collective approach to caring for the 'self' might require. Most of the approaches I have described address only part of the way I have defined care of the 'self', that is they are largely concerned with enhancing the ability to manage one's own health. Independence and autonomy are fostered often with the aim of reducing burden on the system and, through this, reduce costs. I would like to emphasise the personal value of care of the 'self'.

While themes of self-management and client centred care are important, I refer to a broader goal and value system based upon it. That is a system that recognises, values and attends to all its users' sense of 'self' through the ambience it creates, the people working within it, and the therapeutic alliances established with those seeking treatment, care or assistance. Health professionals should value and work with individual self-care practices and act as mentors, assisting and providing for the 'cultivation of self' however this may be pursued. Health professionals should also recognise that care is part of family and kinship groups and that these are the primary forms of caring, the health care that health care professionals provide is at best supplemental.

By referring to ambience I return to my earlier architectural theme. The buildings that house the physical environment of health care need to be completely rethought. Hospital design needs to move away from reflecting and promoting clinical efficiency to buildings that 'write in' and represent the personal, individual choice, comfort, and aesthetics relevant to individuals and to the communities served. Instead of transporting individuals away from their everyday lives into another world, hospitals, surgeries, community health clinics, and other health care institutions should reflect a sense of the everyday and of service, as well as provide the means for self-discovery and self-maintenance. They should let go of the principles of monitoring and control and replace these with systems that facilitate individual voluntary action.

Ambience is created not only through architectural form or interior design: these merely embody, reflect or reinforce a culture created from within. Most importantly ambience is created by the systems and individual actions that comprise health care delivery. All levels of health care, from the systemic through to the myriad face to face encounters that comprise such delivery need to be reviewed and reinvented.

Health care that genuinely values people's 'selves' requires new kinds of personnel, recast as partners (rather than those with authority or in authority) assisting self-action and recognising the need for self-discovery in those who seek out health care. For those people who are unable to care for themselves, health care personnel, skilled as facilitators of self-action, will need to turn outwards a deep knowledge of care of 'self' to its mirrored counterpart – care of others. In both situations new therapeutic alliances are required.

Barker (1997) illuminates something of the nature of new therapeutic alliances that might be forged in the context of psychiatric nursing. He says:

'Brain imaging techniques, human genome mapping and developments in psychopharmacology tell us nothing of the human experience of mental distress…they are of little significance to the practice of nursing, which remains an interpersonal activity enacted within the context of everyday life…People with mental health problems have a problem with their illness, disorder, dysfunction (or whatever). If nurses address anything it is the person's relationship with their illness. The challenge facing psychiatric nurses is not to become more conversant with psychotechnologies, but to develop more sophisticated ways of helping people teach us about their experiences of the human meaning of distress….' (p. 54)

Thus the shape of health care that fulfils this new agenda for care of people's 'selves' is one where health care is opened up to become a resource, and where health carers engage in meaningful therapeutic alliances in order to enhance individual 'self' care, and where those complaints that genuinely lie within the domain of the legitimate activity of biomedicine, are also given a place. The exact boundaries of these aspects of health care have yet to be fully explored, and remain untested. The domain of biomedicine is forever moving forwards to embrace further areas of the body and individual lives. In each instance where this arises it is equally important to study carefully how individual resources may be employed to manage or cope with the distress and difficulty imposed by ill health or its treatment; where legitimate alternatives exist to biomedical approaches these should be valued and promoted alongside traditional forms of management.

Argument has been made for the use of alternative approaches such as meaning or narrative centred care. Here an individual's story of illness is valued. The telling of one's story, which is shared and retold by a skilled health professional in order to affirm an individual's ability to cope, is believed to have great therapeutic potential. It is, however, currently relegated to a secondary position, after biomedical management, to be attempted when all else has failed, for example in chronic pain (Kleinman 1988). My own research into breathlessness, a severe and difficult symptom of advanced lung cancer lies in this area. Together with colleagues, I have demonstrated that even in extreme imminently life-threatening illness, where a gross physical problem such as a tumour of the lung exists, illness can be effectively addressed through narrative and meaning centred care coupled with the facilitation of skills in self-management. Care, however, needs to be offered in the context of a therapeutic alliance quite different from that offered by conventional biomedical approaches.

Benner and Gordon (1996) differentiate between caring, and caregiving as a set of concrete caring practices. They recognise that most doctors or other health professionals for that matter, 'really care about their patients', that is they care deeply about what happens to them and want them to get better, to be cured of their illness. This generalised sentiment is quite different from caregiving. They contrast this general sentiment with the actions of a doctor colleague who has deliberately established a set of practices that allow him to connect with and get to know patients; he establishes a caring frame in which to do his work. He never overbooks his clinic so that he speeds between patients waiting in separate clinic rooms; he gives his patients all the time they need, he lets them talk without interrupting them or directing the conversation into areas that suit him rather than them. When visiting a ward he asks the nurse who has been with the patient how they are, when there is hands-on care to be given he helps the nurse rather than leaves this to her.

He puts aside time to be with patients when there are no longer things to be done for them:

'He has created a setting in which caring can take place and a style of being and communication that implicitly and explicitly tells the patient that they are if not more important than he is, at least as important....Contrast this with many other physicians who deny the space for more than cursory conversation and brief encounters that primarily centre around advice giving: a doctor with an office full of patients, booked four per fifteen minute slot, who must each endure one to three hour waits before they even get on to the exam rooms, juggling two or three more cases in his head; a doctor who, with body language, and impatient verbal interruptions signals the patient has gotten 'off track' because he or she is talking about what has meaning for the patient rather than for the doctor...This physician may want the best for his patients intellectually but has created an environment in which caregiving is impossible' (p42)

This version of health care is not simply the result of an overstretched system that creates lack of caregiving, lack of attention to people's 'selves', we have choices, unfortunately too often we choose to neglect the alternatives.

The challenge is to create a system in which the needs of individuals are addressed in the context of highly sophisticated and technologically advanced biomedicine, and equally sophisticated caregiving practices that sustain people's 'selves' are valued and promoted. Such a system should also connect with and support people to foster their own health and, should the need arise, to manage illness and its effects themselves, harnessing health care commodities, information and supportive communication as well as the array of technologies that are, and will become available.

Here we have travelled full circle. Paradoxically, the dominance of biomedicine, together with other social trends, have led to the possibility of creating a new culture: a culture of preoccupation with 'self' and with it the desire for self-care. Now it is time to harness this impending revolution within health care itself. To reshape health care from a system characterised by dominance and control into one that embodies service and facilitation, an open system that invites participation in its physical representation and in the caring practices it offers. Such a system would not be preoccupied with determining what is 'good' for people, since people should determine this themselves, but would instead provide the resources and support for this self-determination. One could envisage a 'health care lounge', openly accessible, where people themselves determine which of a number of routes they might take. This would be a service without gatekeepers, in which the moment when a diagnosis is identified is jointly determined and supported by health professionals and the person who is ill before joint decisions are made about which route might be taken to manage or resolve health related problems.

Illness, disease and suffering will continue to be the central focus of health care; they should be embraced, acknowledged and assisted within a highly technologically advanced system, but treatment and care should be delivered through caring practices equally celebrated for their success in supporting people, acknowledging distress and aiding recovery.

7. Conclusions

Given the task of reviewing health care, a futurologist, much in vogue in corporate life, would fashion something very different. A selection of scenarios would be presented, suggesting different versions of the predicted future, the goal being to create the future by making clear its possibilities and to take steps to avoid threats that may loom on the horizon. In contrast, much of what I have written draws on the past and I explore its influences in the present to explain how things have become, and how the status quo is powerfully maintained by the present. I have argued that central is the relationship between health care and people who make use of it, and yet currently this relationship is neglected, relegated to the status of unimportant, secondary to the more heroic goal of curing disease.

Through the exploration of a number of themes I have attempted to illuminate the complexities of recasting this relationship since it is not simply about the nature of single encounters with health care professionals or enabling individuals to take more control. Through the stories of Mike and Simon, and Frank Muir's humour, a powerful sense of inhumanity enshrined in health care situations is evoked. This is curious since health care is founded on the most profoundly benevolent of values and aspirations. Social forces are and will bring about evolution and change, however the result of this is unpredictable because it is unplanned. For this reason I have, perhaps unwisely, stepped out of the reflective mode I chose for this monograph. For the penultimate chapter I have proposed 'self' care and care of people's 'selves' as a guiding value for future health care planning. Also to develop a deeper understanding of the caregiving practices that are required in order to foster the sense of receiving such care. This may have been at the risk of presenting a utopian vision for health care, something quite out of keeping with the task I set myself or the perspectives of those who have influenced me. In order to achieve the kind of reorientation I propose, all those engaged in health care need to pursue ways in which it might be more possible for people to retain their 'me-ness'; to be themselves when encountering formal health care. To achieve this policy makers need to explore how:

- The boundary between formal and informal care might be expanded into a fluid and flexible intermediate 'grey' territory and where such a territory exists in formal health care settings, consider how this might be jointly 'owned' by people and professionals.

- Within the more solid settings of formal health care, an environment more familiar to people's everyday lives might be created. Where caring and 'self' care is valued equally to treatment and science, and where those providing care are less preoccupied with their career and status.

- Finally, develop architecture for health care that reflects and promotes the goals and philosophy of the people focused activities that take place within.

The reason for proposing such change is not to effect a revolution, but simply to encourage a refashioning of health care so that it more closely reflects contemporary society. If this fails to occur, one can expect an increasing display of public dissatisfaction, distrust and possibly fragmentation of a system that to date has been loved as a pillar of collective social identity. Alternatively, to achieve such change might indeed be liberating for all concerned, opening up new avenues for health care and the Health Service, for resolving current tensions and difficulties.

REFERENCES

Alberts J.F., Sanderman R., Gerstenbluth I., Wim J.A., van den Heuvel W. (1998) Sociocultural variations in help-seeking behaviour for every day symptoms and chronic disorders. Health Policy, 44, 57-72.

Ameri A. (1998) On the art of spacing. Semiotica 121, 3/41, 283-301.

Armstrong D. (1994) Bodies of knowledge/knowledge of bodies in C. Jones and R. Porter (eds). Reassessing Foucault: Power, medicine and the body. London. Routledge.

Armstrong D. (1995) The rise of surveillance medicine. Sociology of Health and Illness. 17 (3), 393-404.

Barker P. (1998) Advanced practice in mental health nursing: developing the core. In Rolfe G. and Fulbrook R. (eds). Advanced Nursing Practice. Oxford. Butterworth/Heinemann.

Barthes R. (1986) Semiology and the Urban, The City and the Sign. M.Gottidiener and A. Lagopoulos (eds) New York: Columbia University Press p.88-89. Reprinted with minor amendments in Leach N. (1997) Rethinking architecture. London. Routledge.

Bataille G. (1930) Museum. Translated by Paul Hogarty. Original text 'musèe', Pictionnaire Critique, 1930, 5, p.300. Reprinted in Leach N. (1997) ed. Rethinking Architecture. London. Routledge.

Benner P. and Gordon S. (1996) Caring Practice. In S. Gordon, P. Benner and N. Noddings (eds) Caregiving: readings in knowledge, practice, ethics and politics. Philadelphia. University of Pennsylvania Press.

Bunton R and Peterson A. (1997) eds. Foucault, Health and Medicine. London. Routledge, p 3-4.

Bunton R. (1997) Popular health and advanced liberalism. In R. Bunton and A. Peterson (eds). Foucault, health and medicine. London. Routledge.

Chewning B. and Sleath B. (1996) Medication decision-making and management: A client centred model. Social Science and Medicine, 42(3), 389-397.

Cutler S. (1996) A Survivor's Tale. The Pharos. Spring, 36-40.

Dargie C. (1999) Policy Futures for UK Health: Pathfinder, London. The Nuffield Trust.

Davies C. (1995) Competence versus care? Gender and caring work revisited. Acta Sociologica. 38, 17-31.

Davies C. (1996) The sociology of professions and the profession of gender. Sociology, 30(4), 661-678.

Dean K. (1986) Lay care in illness. Social Science and Medicine, 22, 275

Department of Health (1998) A first class service: Quality in the new NHS, DOH, Leeds.

Department of Health (2000). The NHS Plan. London. HMSO.

Foucault M. (1975) Discipline and Punish. London. Allen Lane.

Foucault M. (1977) Panopticism, Discipline and Punish. New York. Vintage Books.

Foucault M. (1984/1991) On the Genealogy of Ethics: An overview of work in progress. In P. Rainbow (ed) The Foucault Reader. London. Penguin.

Foucault M. (1986/1963) Birth of the Clinic. London. Routledge (pxviii-xix).

Foucault M. (1986/1990) The Care of the Self. Translated by Robert Hurley. London. Penguin.

Foucault M. (1989/1967) Madness and Civilization: A history of insanity in the age of reason. Translated by Richard Howard. London. Routledge, p271-2.

Francis S., Glanville R., Noble A. and Scher P. (1999) 50 Years of Ideas in Health Care Buildings. London. The Nuffield Trust.

Frankenburg A. (1992) Your Time or Mine: temporal contradictions of biomedical practice. In R Frankenburg (ed) Time, Health and Medicine. London. Sage.

Frankenburg R. (1998) Your Time or Mine: an anthropological account of the tragic contradictions of biomedical practice. International Journal of Health Services. 18(1), 11-34.

Gamarnikov E. (1978) Sexual division of labour: The case of nursing. In A. Kuhn and A M Wolpe (eds) Feminism and Materialism: women and modes of production. London. Routledge and Kegan Paul.

Giddens A (1991) Modernity and Self-identity: self and society in the late modern age. Stanford. Stanford Press.

Goffman E. (1968) Asylums: Essays on the social situations of mental patients and other inmates. London. Penguin.

Hamon C. (1998) Some NHS care is unacceptable. Personal view. British Medical Journal, 317: 1463.

Haug M.R. (1973) Deprofessionalization: an alternative hypothesis for the future. Sociological Review Monographs. 20, 195-211.

HMSO (1998) Report of the Health Service Ombudsman for 1996-7.

Hughes J. (1997) Hospital-City. Architectural History. 40, 266-288.

Illich I. (1990/1976) Limits to Medicine, medical nemesis: the expropriation of health. London. Penguin books.

James N. (1989) Emotional labour: skill and work in the regulation of feelings. Sociological Review, 37(1), 15-42.

Jameson F. (1991) The cultural logic of late modern capitalism. London Verso. Reprinted in Leach N (ed) Rethinking Architecture. London. Routledge.

Jones C. and Porter R. (1994) eds. Reassessing Foucault: Power, medicine and the body. London. Routledge, p2.

Kleinman A. (1988) The Illness Narratives: suffering, healing and the human condition. New York. Basic Books.

Kracauer S. (1995) The Hotel Lobby (extract), Mass Ornament, translated by Thomas Lanin, Cambridge, Massachusetts: Harvard University Press. Reprinted in Leach N. (1997) as above. Also, On employment exchanges: the construction of space. Translated by David Frishy, original text: Uber Arbeitsnachweise: Konstruktion eines Rammes, Schriften, Baud 5.2, ed. Inka Mülder-Bach, Frankfurt am Main: Suh-Kampverlag, 1990. Pp. 185-92. Reprinted in Leach N. (1997) as above.

Leach N. (1997) ed: Rethinking Architecture. London. Routledge.

Lupton D. (1997) Foucault and the medicalisation critique. In C. Jones and R. Porter (eds) Reassessing Foucault: Power, medicine and the body. London. Routledge.

Lupton D. (1997) Medicine as Culture: illness, disease and the body in western societies. London. Sage.

May C. (1992) Nursing work, nurses' knowledge and the subjectification of the patient. Sociology of Health and Illness, 14(4), 472-487.

Miewald C. (1997) Is Awareness enough? The Contradictions of self-care in a chronic disease clinic. Human Organisation, 56(3), 353-363.

Muir F. A Kentish lad. BBC Radio 4.

Mumby D K and Putnam L L. (1992) The politics of emotion: A feminist reading of bounded rationality. Academy of Management Review, 17(3), 465-468.

Parson T. (1951) The Social Systems. London. Routledge and Kegan Paul.

Pringle R. (1998) Sex and Medicine: gender, power and authority in the medical profession. Cambridge. Cambridge University Press.

Prior L. (1988) The architecture of the hospital: a study of spatial organisation and medical knowledge. The British Journal of Sociology, xxxix (1), 86-113.

Rafferty A. (1996) The Politics of Nursing Knowledge. London. Routledge.

Rose N. (1994) Medicine, history and the present. In Colin Jones and Roy Porter (eds) Reassessing Foucault: Power, medicine and the body. London. Routledge.

Srnka Q. and Portner S. (1997) Exploring self-care and Wellness: A model for pharmacist compensation by managed care organisations. American Journal of Managed care. 3(6), 943-952.

Stein L I. (1967) The Doctor-nurse game. Archives of General Psychiatry. 16, June, 699-703.

Stein L I., Watts D T and Howell T. (1990) The Doctor-nurse game revisited. Nursing Outlook, 38(6), 264-268.

Steinweg K., Nannini R.J., Killingsworth R.E. and Spayde J. (1998) The Impact on a health care system of a programme to facilitate self-care. Military Medicine, 163(3), 139-144.

Waerness K. (1992) On the rationality of caring. In A. Showstack sesson (ed) Women and the State. London. Routledge.

Williams S., Michie S. and Pattai S. (1998) Improving the Health of the NHS Workforce. London. The Nuffield Trust.

Woolf V. (1928/1945) A Room of One's Own. London. Penguin.

Zola I.K. (1972) Medicine as an institution of social control. Sociological Review. 25, 4, 487-504.

Zola I.K. (1973) Pathways to the Doctor – from person to patient. Social Science and Medicine. 7, 677-689.